Do Pause

You are not a To Do list

Robert Poynton

For my parents

Published by
The Do Book Company 2019
Works in Progress Publishing Ltd
thedobook.co

Text © Robert Poynton 2019
Photography © Jim Marsden 2019

To find out more about our company,
books and authors, please visit
thedobook.co or follow us **@dobookco**

5% of our proceeds from the sale of
this book is given to The DO Lectures
to help it achieve its aim of making
positive change **thedolectures.com**

Cover designed by James Victore
Book designed and set by Ratiotype

Printed and bound by OZGraf Print
on Munken, an FSC® certified paper

MIX
Paper from
responsible sources
FSC® C163799
www.fsc.org

A CIP catalogue record for this book
is available from the British Library

ISBN 978-1-907974-63-2

10 9 8 7 6

Contents

1
Why Pause?

It was a warm Sunday evening in mid-September. I was sitting on the terrace, looking up at the Sierra de Gredos, enjoying dinner and a glass (or two) of red wine with my good friend Chris Riley. We had spent the weekend on the other side of the mountains, hidden away in an ancient house in Avila, with eight other people and dozens of books, reading and talking about what we had read.

'I could do that every year,' said Chris.

So we did.

Since I live in central Spain and Chris is in Oregon, it is hardly convenient. Yet every year, he travels over five thousand miles, for a couple of days, to do very little. Others travel considerable distances too. What is this about? It is about the power of a pause.

That Sunday evening, as we sat and talked, Chris was keenly aware of how much the time-out had given him and how much he'd needed it. Hence his comment. He could feel it had affected him on many levels — physically, mentally and emotionally. He even looked different. The switch of activity and rhythm enabled him to notice and pay attention to what was going on inside him. He found he was able to reconnect with himself, as well as forge new connections with others. His sense of what mattered shifted. It was a moment of resetting, of regeneration, of new ideas and perspectives. It deepened his thinking. Time itself seemed to slow down (or open up) and he found himself 'coming up with ideas to solve problems I didn't know I had' without even trying. What looked like time off enabled him to do work of a different kind.

Chris recognised that this was an ongoing need, not a one-off. It wasn't that he wanted to do it again — he wanted to do it *every* year. His comment was a watershed and the Reading Weekend became an annual fixture in the calendar; a pivotal point that gives shape to a year. For Chris, it is a chance to examine his own thinking from a fresh perspective, in the light of new stimulus; to give his ideas room to breathe. There is anticipation leading up to it and a period of synthesis following it. It might be just a weekend but the effects are significant.

Nonetheless, it had taken me years, and a number of invitations to similar events, to get Chris to come. The idea of stopping can be simultaneously attractive and scary. Even once he got here, allowing himself this short period of undirected time was not straightforward. 'I spent the first twenty-four hours watching my own levels of anxiety rise, because I wasn't working on anything,' he said. This is not unusual. The pressures and habits of everyday work and life can make it hard to pause for a few days, or even for a few seconds.

A pause may be so slight that it is easy to forget, ignore or skip over. In one's enthusiasm to forge ahead, the spaces to notice, or appreciate, or reflect, are often left by the wayside. We are all prey to this. I can easily catch myself filling in the little gaps and spaces in the day, making calls or sending emails. Yet the idea of 'never a wasted moment' comes at a cost. Not long ago, when my sister and her husband visited, I took them on a mountain walk. I noticed they kept stopping. Or to be more accurate, I noticed that I had *stopped* stopping. I often walk on my own, so walking in company made me realise that, over time, I had become almost entirely focused on getting to the top, taking pride in how quickly I could do so. The walk had become a goal to be achieved, rather than an experience to be enjoyed. Yet why bother with a mountain walk if you never pause to take it all in? I was missing the point as well as the view.

How often do we do something like this? For example, our children can easily become just a stream of endless tasks: feeding, dressing, getting them to school or football practice or dance class, doing homework, bedtime story and so on. In the midst of all that, do we allow ourselves time to actually be with them, to enjoy them? Do we give them the time to be childlike, or are we so focused on having them notch up another achievement that they miss out on the 'view' along the way? In general, we don't pay much attention or give much importance to the spaces in between all the tasks. I think we should. In life, as in art, you need to step back to see that. The 'negative space', which lies around or between objects or events, gives shape to the whole.

It is easy to miss this. The space in our lives is always under pressure. There are powerful forces that combine to squeeze it out. First among these is technology. Machines work well at a constant speed — and the faster the better. They are designed and built for it. Whether they are spinning cotton or crunching numbers, regular, repetitive actions are what they excel at and, increasingly, our world is designed by machines, for machines. Yet what works well for machines doesn't work well for people.

The language and imagery we use to describe our relationship with technology is revealing — we talk of 'drowning', feeling 'paralysed' or having to 'detox'. As writer Pico Iyer says: 'The one thing technology cannot give us is a sense of how to make the wisest use of technology.' Yet digital technology intrudes ever more intimately into our lives. We may hold our phones in the palm of our hand, but it is they that have *us* in their grasp.

We find ourselves adapting to machines and hold ourselves to their standards: people are judged by the speed with which they respond, not the quality of their response. Our language and norms evolve to reflect this. 'Always on' becomes something to boast of, or aspire to. Such ideas are being woven into our culture. As more of us dwell in cities with little direct connection to nature, older cultural practices that were more in tune with the ebb and flow of seasons and tides are flattened or lost; buried under an insensible, incessant, machine-driven beat.

We give high status to busy-ness. We have created a sprawling industry of 'personal productivity' and time management, which once again owes a lot to machines, prizing efficiency above all else. The idea that speed equals productivity is so widespread and dominant we are hardly aware of it. Thus we associate pause with delay and procrastination, not deliberation or wisdom.

The twin forces of technology and culture both draw upon and feed a third influence, rooted deep in our psyche. Overwork, or constant work, can be a means of escaping ourselves. It covers a yawning well of anxiety about what might happen if we were to stop. We are fearful of what we might discover. If we are not ticking things off our to-do list, then who are we?

Faced with that anxiety we try to keep calm by carrying on. The confluence of these forces keeps us going relentlessly, even at considerable cost to ourselves. Together, they create a myopic loop that makes it hard to see any other option. We convince ourselves we are indispensable and exist in a state of 'continuous partial attention' where we are constantly interrupted but never consciously pause. To pause becomes taboo.

In recent years the accelerating speed of life has given rise to the 'slow' movement — a natural and healthy response. There is much I enjoy and applaud about this. I regularly attend meals of our local branch of the Slow Food Society. Where I live in rural Spain, the pace of life is slow compared to any city, and that is part of what I like about it. Yet it is simplistic to believe that the answer to this acceleration is just to put the brakes on.

As they are fond of saying in Silicon Valley: 'Today is the slowest day of the rest of your life.' And yet, the sensation of struggling to keep up is not a new phenomenon at all. While the objective speed of communication or travel has increased dramatically, people's subjective response at any point in history is remarkably similar. Thus in 1908 French writer Octave Mirbeau said, 'Everywhere life is rushing insanely like a cavalry charge.' Thirty years earlier, in 1880, Nietzsche was already complaining of a growing culture 'of indecent and perspiring haste'. But even Nietzsche was late to the game. Fifty-five years before that, in a letter to a friend, Goethe said, 'Young people are swept along in the whirlpool of time; wealth and speed are what the world admires and what everyone strives for.' He could have been writing today.

We feel imprisoned by the way we live in time. However fast things may actually be, it seems that people always feel it is too fast. This says as much about us as it does about the world around us. Our sensation of time is much like our sensation of taste. Sensory psychologist Charles Spence says that 'taste is on the tongue, not in the food'. The rosé you try at the chateau in Provence while watching the sun set over the lavender fields tastes great. When you get it home, it doesn't. You are right in both cases. The chateau and the sunset affect you (and your tongue) so that it really does taste different. Something similar happens to us with speed. What we expect, how we prepare, how we feel, prime us to experience pace and time in one way or another. Time is not in the clock, it is in us.

The desire to go more slowly is understandable and has a place, but it is of limited practical use, for a number of reasons. First, it is wishful thinking. As technology accelerates exponentially, the pace of events is not going to slow down. Technology will continue to accelerate, dragging us with it, just as it has for a couple of centuries at least. If you make slowing things down a goal, it sets you up to fail. It also creates tension between how you would like things to be and how they are. Which is precisely the kind of tension that leads to stress.

Second, since speed is always relative, quite what it means to be slow is not necessarily clear. How slow is slow? Today's slow, or tomorrow's? My slow or your slow? What is the standard, or reference point? Is slower always better? If so, then how much should you slow down by? If not, then how do you know when to slow down and when not to? How do you know when slow is too slow? Advocating a single direction of travel, towards slowness, isn't very practical. It ignores the importance of context and counterpoint.

Moreover, if the sensation of speed is in you, then what matters is how you experience and perceive speed and time. Since you can't change the pace of events, it makes more sense to work on how you react to them. Rather than dig your heels in and resist acceleration, it is more intelligent to ask how you can respond creatively to it.

The idea of 'work-life balance' doesn't help either. It sets up work and life as opposites, squabbling over their fair share of time. The importance we give to work makes it an unequal battle and, more often than not, what we refer to as 'life' gets squeezed. But there is a more fundamental problem here. The sharp distinction between work and life misrepresents both. On the one hand, any work worth doing has some kind of life or liveliness in it — no amount of time off can possibly make up for 'deathly' work. On the other hand, there is plenty that we have to work at outside the office, in the intimate space of our own lives — personal relationships spring to mind as one immediate example.

Fast versus slow, and work versus life, are, in fact, bogus choices. In setting up one against the other, we miss the fact that there are other, less combative, possibilities. We ignore the value of variation and modulation. Which is where pause comes into its own. Pause is part of work and life. It isn't fast or slow. It doesn't exist at a single point on the spectrum of speed, but all over it. Whatever you may be doing and whatever speed you are moving at, there is always the chance to pause.

Helene Simonsen is a classical musician. Since her instrument is the flute, there has to be pause in everything she plays, in order for her to breathe. For her, breathing is part of the music. Some composers signal where to pause and breathe, but with others (Bach in particular, she says) you have to find or make the space to pause for yourself. Pause is something that the musician, and the music, cannot do without. As Helene says, 'Whatever you are doing, if you want something else to happen, you need to pause.'

Without a pause, everything continues as it was. Even something as mechanical as changing gear in a car is smoother when you add the tiniest of pauses in neutral, between gears. Pausing is part of living and breathing. Indeed, between breathing in and breathing out, there's a pause. The purpose of having a break isn't only to rest, important though that may be. As Helene says, it allows something else to occur: 'my playing often develops through the breaks'. In a pause you can question existing ways of acting, have new ideas or simply appreciate the life you are living. Without ever stopping to observe yourself, how can you explore what else you might do or who you might become? If you always head on relentlessly, where is the room for the heart?

A life without pause is unhealthy, from the cellular level up. It profoundly affects how we feel. If you don't stop to think, life will force you to stop and think. At the extreme, the cost is 'burnout'. It is a striking image; of being consumed by fire. These days burnout is increasingly common, especially among those people we think of and label as 'successful' — a fact which, surely, ought to give us pause for thought.

That isn't the only risk. When people burn out, it is crippling, but at least it is dramatic enough to demand attention. It forces reconsideration. Burnout can be seen as 'a sane reaction to an insane world', a response that comes from some buried inner wisdom, reasserting itself in a highly conspicuous way. Less extreme but more insidious is the slow, suffocating smoulder. As we constantly push on from one task to the next, we can become our 'to-do' lists. Little by little, we learn to live with less of ourselves. It is death by a thousand meetings. What we could be becomes a forgotten dream.

As well as the cost to our health or sanity, there is the

cost of what you miss along the way. Fail to pause and you miss out on the view, or the path not taken. What's more likely to get your kids to talk to you: questioning them or allowing them some space? With no pause (or silence) in a meeting, you may rattle through the agenda, but fail to tackle the underlying issues. What other more creative, more powerful conversations might you have, if only you were able to let a bit of daylight into the process? What deeper questions might be raised? What other voices might you hear? As you bowl along, are you really thinking or are you just reacting? Is packing more in really the way to do your best work, or to get the most out of life?

Pausing to think about what we do also matters in the moral dimension. If you never stop to question what you are doing, how will you know you are doing a good thing? It may be rational and efficient for tax accountants to keep developing products and services to meet their clients' needs (i.e. help them pay less tax) or for social-media platforms to seek ever more eyeballs, but if they never pause to consider the broader implications of what they do, it shouldn't be a surprise if they end up in morally dubious territory.

The kind of work we do and the nature of the problems we face require more pause, not less. As journalist Carl Honoré says: 'Many modern jobs depend on the kind of creative thinking that seldom occurs at a desk and cannot be squeezed into a fixed schedule.' A similar argument applies on a global scale.

At Oxford, Ian Goldin, Professor of Globalisation and Development, argues that we need to stand back and contemplate the complex world we live in, if we want to understand how to act in it. Columnist Tom Friedman has a similar view: 'Opting to pause and reflect, rather than panic or withdraw, is a necessity ... not a luxury or a distraction.' Pause is thus an active presence; not so much an absence of thought or action, as an integral part of it.

Time, they say, is a scarce commodity. Underlying this idea is the morbid but unavoidable truth that, one day, we all die. A common response to this is to try and cram in as much as possible while we are here. This is understandable and often unconscious. It is particularly strong in the modern, industrialised West, where the feeling of time scarcity, coupled with the Protestant work ethic, contributes to the popularity of life hacks and productivity tips.

Yet there is more to life than getting things done. Time isn't a commodity at all, scarce or otherwise; it isn't a uniform, undifferentiated, raw material (even to a physicist, there is more to time than that, as we shall see). Time, as we experience it, is wildly different, depending on what we are doing. A minute waiting for the bus is not the same as a minute doing press-ups or a minute savouring the taste of ice cream. A year at work is not comparable to a year spent travelling. We may have a limited amount of time available to us in this life, as measured by the clock; but you are not a clock.

I want to invite you to let go of the idea that time is linear, regular and objective, and think of it in the same way we experience it — as elastic, variable and layered. I am not so interested in how you cram more in to your life, but in how you get more out. To do so may require all sorts of strategies, but one thing I am sure of: it entails being able to pause.

A pause is an opening. It acts as a portal to other options and choices, giving more dimension to your experience. Just as a small amount of yeast makes light of heavy dough, a small amount of pause here and there can leaven or lighten your life. You don't need much but it is a vital ingredient.

A book is a medium that lends itself to pausing — you get to choose when to dwell on something, when to re-read a sentence, or when to put the book down, which is one of the joys of reading. So while you will find lots of ideas about pausing in this book, you don't need to wait until you have finished it; you could stop reading right here, right now ... and pause. You might ask yourself why you were drawn to this book, and take a few moments to contemplate what it is about the idea of pause that attracted you. Or you might take that moment to enjoy the view, or notice how you feel, or let your mind wander. The book will still be here for you later, to pick up again whenever you wish.

Experimenting with pause gives you a way to play around with the rhythms of your life. It gives you a way to give shape and texture to your experience, weakening the sensation that your life is driven by external forces over which you have no influence. Choosing where you put your pauses makes an enormous difference to what your life feels like and what you can do as a result.

You might pause to rest and regenerate, to become more creative, to connect with other people or yourself, or just to enjoy whatever it is that is going on around you (or inside you). There are many possible reasons to pause, ways to pause and lengths of pause. There are many different practices you can adopt. You can play around to your heart's desire and choose whatever suits you: pause is quite the opposite of a task to tick off. Pause is a very plastic concept. There is plenty to try, as we will see. It is a subtle, powerful, life-giving idea — one that is worth spending a little time with.

A pause is an opening.
It acts as a portal to other
options and choices,
giving more dimension
to your experience

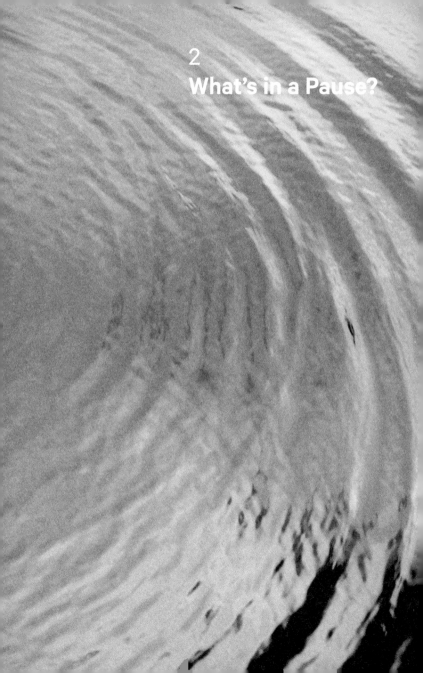

2
What's in a Pause?

A pause is a curious thing. It seems so simple and familiar, yet dwell on it for a moment or two and you start to realise that there is more to it than meets the eye (or the ear). For example, if I ask you how long is a pause, what would you say? It seems a simple question at first, yet would you be able to provide a simple answer with any precision or conviction? Would your response be the same as mine? Would your answer ever change? Though we know a pause when we see one, we can't be so sure how long it might be; it is not a defined, regular, fixed unit of time.

This question also demonstrates that a pause can have many different effects. By inviting you to 'dwell' on something (i.e. pause) I drew your attention to it. That allowed you to examine a familiar idea (in this case 'pause' itself) and, perhaps, shifted your perspective. So a pause isn't only about having a rest, it can do a variety of things.

There are different kinds of pause with different uses and benefits. There are dramatic or pregnant pauses. You might pause for effect or pause for thought. A pause can be planned or spontaneous, momentary or lasting. A pause might help you to prepare for something that is going to happen, or to make sense of something that already has. Pause is important to creativity, communication and relationships. It is also important to your own wellbeing and sanity. You might pause to get organised, add emphasis, connect with others, get a new perspective, exercise judgement and so on — it's a long list. With such variety on offer, the opportunity is there to become a connoisseur of pauses. This multi-faceted nature is what makes pause worth exploring. It is a rich, layered, nuanced phenomenon. Empty though it may seem, there's a lot in a pause.

The aim of this chapter is to explore that complex nature. Far from defining it, which reduces or limits our understanding, I want to expand it. I want to flesh out the concept of pause, to unpack it and celebrate its riches and its subtlety.

Though I referred to pause as a 'curious thing', that's a trap that language lays for us. A pause is not a thing at all. It is an opening which allows, enables, permits or invites all sorts of other possibilities. These are very gentle, generous verbs: allow, enable, permit, invite. Pause does not demand, command or control. It allows something to happen which would otherwise not occur, and you never quite know what that will be.

So, what is a pause? It clearly has something to do with time, but, as we have seen, even the outwardly simple question 'How long is a pause?' is hard to answer. In different contexts a pause could perfectly well be three seconds, or ten, or thirty; but pauses can also occur at different levels of scale altogether. You could pause for a moment in a conversation or meeting: a few silent seconds that speak volumes. Or you could put something aside for an hour or two while you go for a walk. Or you could take a few days once a year, like the reading retreat; or an entire year, in the form of a sabbatical. A pause can exist for a few seconds, minutes, hours, days, years or longer. Though they have very different durations, we happily recognise all of these as pauses.

A pause interrupts something, but it doesn't stop there. The effects of a pause go beyond the duration of the pause itself; it doesn't have sharp edges. Artist Tom Hiscocks describes pause as a marinade, leaving a 'flavour' that you can detect afterwards. For him, pausing regularly 'creates a resource that can be tapped into … you know it's there, you can go back to it at any time, even in the midst of activity'. Thus a pause can continue to nourish you, even when it is behind you. Similarly, when a pause you have planned is ahead of you, it can act as a 'forward anchor'. The knowledge that it is coming helps keep you steady through frenetic periods. The effects of a pause can start early and stay late.

A pause is something you sink into, even if only for a moment. It is distinct from the ping of an email, or an impatient listener interrupting in the middle of a sentence. It comes from within, not without, and is often chosen or conscious.

Is pause about slowing down? Sometimes it is, but not always. As the saying goes, 'more haste, less speed'. This suggests that hasty action — i.e. action without any pause — can be slower. I see this in my work with improvisational theatre. Most people assume that improv theatre is about thinking fast, but in fact it is novices that rush; skilled improvisers know how to pause. This may be imperceptible to the audience, yet the pauses are necessary to make the story flow, they allow the players to give space to each other and work together effectively. Thus, contrary to what we might expect, being able to pause can make things flow faster.

We see this offstage too. A leader who senses when to pause can make people feel secure and calm even in the midst of mayhem; she has presence. The best 'ultra-fast' sports players (like tennis players or cricketers) owe their prowess to being able to pause for the tiniest fraction of a second as the ball approaches. Knowing how and when to pause is the essence of timing.

Pause has a complex and varied relationship with time. It operates outside the fixed and limited measures of the clock. It isn't necessarily slow; but nor is it always fast. A pause can be helpful whatever speed you are going; it has more to do with rhythm than pace, it is more a question of timing than of time. It is a quality that infuses a period of time not a unit of time. Pausing allows you to develop different strategies of how to use time; a welcome alternative to constant hurry.

A pause is not nothing. Something happens in a pause, or as a result of one. Thus, pausing is different from stopping. Improviser Gary Hirsch describes it as 'a quality of stopping that makes another kind of thinking possible'. Film-maker David Keating talks about a pause as a 'sweet emptiness'. At a material level, it simply isn't possible for there to be nothing happening, even in a pause. As choreographer and yoga teacher Kay Scorah points out, to stand very still you need to be constantly moving, making tiny adjustments to posture and position. Such 'stillness' is compelling to watch, as the street entertainers posing as statues in cities all over the world demonstrate. Look closely and there is always something going on. When you pause you are still thinking, breathing, metabolising.

Even in meditation, there is not nothing. For meditation teacher Rachel Lebus, stilling or emptying the mind is not the aim; meditation is not an instrument of control.

Images and thoughts inevitably arise, and the meditation consists of letting them go; not of not having them. In meditation there may be a different quality of mind, but the mind is not entirely empty or still. There is not nothing.

Composer John Cage's most famous and controversial work is entitled *4'33"*. In this piece the performer, or performers, are instructed not to play (for four minutes and thirty-three seconds). Cage's point is that there is never complete silence, that 'everything we do is music'. Similarly, pause is not an absence, but an opportunity to be present to what we would otherwise miss or ignore, in the same way that during *4'33"* the 'music' of the background noise that surrounds us all the time appears. A pause, rather than being nothing, is a switch of attention and activity, from one thing to another. It is 'a "not doing" in order for something else to be done', says actor and singer Phyllida Hancock. We may absent ourselves from the usual stuff, but as we do so, we pay attention to something else.

There is a conundrum here, which points, again, to the difference between people and machines. Author and columnist Dov Seidman sums it up beautifully: 'When you press the pause button on a machine it stops. But when you press the pause button on human beings, they start.'

Creativity

Since you never know what it is that might start, pause makes an important contribution to creativity. There are patterns to creative processes. One of the patterns that people who study creativity observe is that there is always a discontinuity, or gap, or delay. In short — a pause.

For example, in *Where Good Ideas Come From*, Steven Johnson talks of the 'slow hunch'. He argues that new ideas are 'fragile creatures, easily lost to the more pressing needs of day-to-day issues'. Slow hunches don't develop if you work relentlessly on a problem. They are 'less a matter of perspiration than cultivation' and, like a crop, require fallow periods. It is a living process, not a mechanical one.

Creative director Jack Foster, in *How to Get Ideas*, is explicit about this. He has 'Forget about it' as one of the stages of his idea-generation process. He cites fellow ad man James Webb Young's 1934 classic *A Technique for Producing Ideas*, as well as the German philosopher Helmholtz and a number of academic researchers. All of them include a stage of disconnection from the task at hand. They may call it 'mental digestion' or 'incubation' but the creative process, however you look at it, has some kind of pause built into it. You don't get to novelty directly.

Often, it is in the pause that the 'eureka moments' occur. These days more people seem to have their ideas in the shower than the bath, but that probably just reflects the change in bathing habits. The drama of the 'eureka' moments makes for a good story, so sudden inspiration often gets most of the attention, but without the pregnant pause that gave birth to them, there would be no such moments at all.

This pattern doesn't only occur with conscious acts of creation. A pause creates space for opportunities of all sorts. Take travel, for example. What seems like dead time often leads to the most compelling experiences. This happened to me in the windswept town of Uyuni, in Bolivia. I arrived quite early and was wandering around, feeling too lazy to find a hotel, when I bumped into Jacques, a Frenchman I had met on the bus. 'There's a truck leaving for the Salar [salt flats] in fifteen minutes,' he said. 'For six dollars they will take us to Chile. Do you want to come?' Had I found a hotel instead of loitering aimlessly, I would have missed everything that followed: the salt flats, the stars seen from an altitude of nearly 4000m, drinking schnapps with the Chilean border police, the British cyclists that appeared like a hallucination out of the desert, bathing in a hot spring with a condor overhead, and so on. No pause, no such possibility.

Uyuni wasn't unique. My life has been shaped by serendipitous moments that happened in an 'in-between' time. I met my wife on a day when a tube strike had paralysed the city of Madrid. Hanging out in Portland, Oregon, for no particular reason, led to me starting a business. Such 'radical serendipities' don't happen when you are head down, rushing to a predetermined destination, or buried up to your eyebrows in everyday detail. The opportunities might still be there, but chances are you won't see or notice them, and even if you do, you are likely to dismiss them as impossible while you speed along the path you have planned. As my friend Jorge Alvarez puts it: 'motorways always lead to known destinations'.

The power of silence

Your pauses have an impact on the people around you, so as well as influencing your capacity for creativity, they affect your relationships. In my work as a facilitator, I have come to cherish silence. It is such a simple form of pause that has such dramatic effects. Just as 'nature abhors a vacuum', people tend to be uncomfortable with silence, so they will break it — sooner or later. Which gives you something to work with. You don't know what they will give you, but if you give them the space, they will always give you something back. The same applies when you appeal for volunteers for improv games. I am often asked:

'What do you do when no one volunteers?' The truth is, I don't know. In twenty years it has never happened. If you are happy to wait, someone always steps up.

The delight of this kind of pause is that all you need is the courage to keep the space open. One of my favourite questions when facilitating (or coaching) is: 'So ...?' This isn't exactly a question but the pause makes it into one, and a beautifully open one at that. It is a question to which almost any response will do. Which makes it perfect when you want to find out what people really want to talk about or when you don't know what to do. You need to be both gentle and patient (tone matters), but if you are, you always learn something. This wouldn't be much use to a lawyer in a court, or anyone with a narrow agenda, but if you want to learn about the people you are working with, or get ideas from them, it is invaluable. The pause does the work for you. You just have to be happy to hold it.

A question of timing

Pause also creates the rhythms of speech, rhythms which are 'as distinctive as thumb prints' (Peter Brook, *The Empty Space*). Performers know this: business people often don't. Phyllida Hancock says: 'As a performer, time, or timing, is the material you work with. We have so many options of how we speak to one another and it's all done with breathing and voice.' If you ever make presentations — take note. The material you are working with is the timing, as much as the slides.

The difference in timing can be tiny. When a film director pauses for an extra three or four seconds before the word 'action' the effect is enormous. The attention of actors and crew is heightened and intensified by the simple addition of a few extra seconds: 'the space of a breath or two'. Poet David Whyte, when leading workshops, will every so often repeat a phrase, particularly when reciting poetry. He will repeat a phrase, particularly when reciting poetry (see what I did there?) This allows the audience to catch up in their listening and invites them to consider the words he repeated a little more deeply.

When I visited Robben Island, where Nelson Mandela was incarcerated, I was shown around by Vincent Dida, who had himself been in jail there for eleven years. Meeting him was by far the most powerful part of the visit, so when we came to leave, I did something I rarely do. 'Would you mind if I had a photo taken with you?' I asked. 'No,' he said firmly, in a very serious tone, and paused. My mind raced. Had I offended him? I felt ashamed and embarrassed. How stupid of me to ask, I thought, he must be sick of being treated like a fairground attraction ... The pause, which felt like forever, ended with him bursting into laughter. 'No,' he repeated, and this time he smiled: 'I wouldn't mind at all.' There is a photo of us, Vincent beaming, me with tears running down my cheeks.

A short pause can do a lot. It draws attention. It creates expectation and suspense. It adds weight. It can say something in its own right. In a narrative it can build up tension or switch you from one story, or point of view, to another. Which is why some playwrights (like some composers) indicate where the actor should pause in the text. They know that the pause will lead the audience and change the meaning. This is why we have punctuation. Without it, you wouldn't know what people meant. Writer Lynne Truss says: 'For a millennium and a half, punctuation's purpose was to guide actors, chanters and readers-aloud through stretches of manuscript, indicating the pauses, accentuating matters of sense and sound.'

She demonstrates this in the very title of her book on punctuation: *Eats, Shoots and Leaves* (try taking the comma out).

How you pause says something about who you are. For example, if you don't ever pause, what does that suggest? Are you scared to stop? Frightened of what people might ask? Worried you won't get the chance to speak again? Some politicians or other public figures actively avoid pausing and try to snatch a breath in the middle of a phrase so that there is no natural break at the end of the sentence for anyone to intervene which means they are able to just keep talking in a desperate attempt to block other people and retain control so they can get to their next prepared talking point. (Phew!) How does that make you feel? Do you trust them? Or warm to them?

Les McKeown, author of *Do Lead*, told me about one of his clients, a CEO who consciously does the opposite. When talking to employees he makes it a practice to yield the last word. At the end of a talk or meeting, instead of hammering home his 'message', he will ensure he leaves a space, which he gives back to the room, so that someone else can have the final say. This is an act of openness and generosity that people notice and appreciate. A pause can be a gift.

A story is told about Alfred Sloan, the CEO of General Motors in its heyday, who used pause to great effect. Sloan was well aware that people would agree with him because of his powerful position, so at a board meeting he said, 'I trust we are all in agreement?' Everyone nodded. 'Then I suggest that we end the meeting and reconvene in two weeks, to give ourselves time to generate some constructive disagreement.' Sloan was aware of the problem of 'yes men' (in the jargon called 'destructive assent'). He used a pause to generate the opposite: 'constructive dissent'.

Percussionist and improviser Thomas Sandberg sees something similar in his performances. For Sandberg, pause is an integral 'musical ingredient' but he also sees it as a chance 'to introduce a little bit of chaos' by creating space for the audience to contribute. This provides a creative input akin to the 'constructive dissent' in Sloan's meetings. It also creates a connection between the performer and his audience.

The connection with an audience often comes through a pause. Zen teacher Edward Espe Brown likes to open up a space at the beginning of a talk. He says: 'I assume that when I get here and meet all of you, right away you are in me and I am in you, and we are quite intimately meeting ... and first I try to listen to you, and sense what you are interested in, so that what I say might be appropriate.'

Having heard Ed talk many times, I noticed that he often just stops, or interrupts himself. His talks are littered with impromptu pauses, which is very endearing and often quite funny. I asked him about this. 'Oh yes,' he said, laughing. 'It's a whole style.'

'Unhurried Conversations' is another whole style (see Resources). It was started by Johnnie Moore and Antony Quinn, both friends of mine and fellow improvisers, to create a space for a different rhythm of interaction. The conversations are held in a café, open to anyone and are governed by a few simple rules.

As Johnnie says, 'We pick an everyday object, like a sugar bowl, and whoever holds it gets to talk. Everyone else listens, so the speaker won't get interrupted, and if they want to, they can hold silence until they're ready to speak. When they are finished, they return the object to the table, and someone else takes a turn. Sometimes there are long pauses between speakers, sometimes not.

'When people know they aren't going to be interrupted, they worry less and express themselves more clearly.' People who attend talk about the sense of connection that is created, even with strangers.

It is fascinating how a pause, which seems to be almost nothing, affects the connections between us so profoundly. Perhaps it isn't surprising. Without words, we are able to connect in other ways. This is important for singers or musicians who, with or without a conductor, use what you might call a 'gathering' pause. They can't just start, first they need to collect and connect their energy and attention, and signal to each other that they are about to go. If they don't do this, they won't be together. To start well, you might need to pause first.

There are obvious benefits of pause to your own wellbeing and sanity. This is an old idea; we know that 'all work and no play' makes for a dull life. Yet, as we saw in the previous chapter, the pressure of modern life means it is a lesson we have to keep learning. It is breaking a taboo when a CEO like Andrew Mackenzie of BHP (one of Australia's largest companies) publicly says 'a rested Andrew can do more in four hours than a tired Andrew in eight'. Similarly, film director Dan Petrie's top tip to people starting out in the trade was nothing technical or creative. It was: 'get to bed before ten'.

Important though rest and regeneration may be, there are a wealth of other personal benefits. A pause is sometimes necessary to allow you to exercise your skill and judgement. Another film director, John Boorman, pauses while shooting so that he can bring his attention to his 'instincts'. A doctor, in the midst of an operation, might pause for a couple of seconds, her finger on the carotid artery, in order to feel and sense the pulse, and make a critical decision about which of two drugs to administer. Access to these other intelligences requires our normal way of thinking to be quiet. Pause gives you access to capacities you might not know you have.

A pause can also help you to understand yourself better. On one retreat we asked people to spend a couple of hours outdoors in contemplation of a landscape. This was effectively a pause (the contemplation) within a pause (the retreat). One of the participants, who had recently left the corporate world, came back asking: 'What if I think of my work, or career, as a field, not a path?' This image gave him a completely different way to think about his work and how it might evolve.

Paradoxically, there are times when a pause offers the opposite of clarity ... and that can be just what you need. The poet John Keats famously spoke of 'negative capability', which he described as the capacity 'of being in uncertainties, mysteries, doubts, without any irritable reaching after fact and reason'. This is hard to do without pausing. So creating a space, be it an hour or a day, where you allow yourself to be in doubt is a way of productively engaging with uncertainty. As my Oxford colleague Tracey Camilleri says: 'Flailing around in doubt is such an important part of finding direction.'

When I started to investigate and play around with pause I was surprised by what fruitful territory it was. It seemed such a simple idea, yet as I started reading and investigating I kept discovering more subtleties and nuances.

In the past couple of years I have spoken to an A to Z of different kinds of people about pause, from actors to zen ministers: including businessmen, choreographers, diplomats, executive coaches, film directors, improvisers, musicians, scientists, teachers, writers and yoga teachers.

They were fascinating conversations. People spoke about knowing how a pause feels, but not being able to say what it is. They use descriptors like 'outside of time' or 'white space'. They talked of silent pauses, pregnant pauses, connective pauses, creative pauses, synchronising pauses and of a pause that leads somewhere in its own right. They asked new and interesting questions that I hadn't thought of — everything from 'Can you pause by accident?' to 'What happens when a whole nation pauses?' They talked about pause in all sorts of contexts including music, drama, television, religion, education, architecture and conversation.

There are so many angles. It is a subtle, unfolding subject, which you can explore endlessly and play around with to your heart's content. I like this. The more I learn about it, the more I feel I have to learn. The more I try to work with it, the more there is to practise. Which is where we are going now.

3
Habits

One of the nicest things about pause is how obvious and familiar it is. You don't need to go to a class or subscribe to any particular beliefs in order to understand it or start working with it. Anyone can think about where or how pauses show up, or are absent, in their own life or work without any prior knowledge or instruction. Pausing is very do-able, which is why it is a good subject for a book in this series.

Meditation, yoga, tai chi and mindfulness are all lovely in their own ways and I am fond of each of them. But they do come with a bit of 'wu-wu' (as Nick Parker, writer and wordsmith, puts it), which can be a distraction or a barrier. Even if, like me, you are partial to a little 'wu-wu' every now and then, you still need a bit of instruction, language or technique in order to get going.

Not so with pause.

Yet for all its ordinariness, as we have seen, pause has variety, depth and complexity. In this sense pause is like wine. Everyone understands what wine is (some of us rather too well) but within the category of wine, there are an infinite number of varieties. I like this. It means everyone can find their own way to pause. You can think about what is interesting or appropriate for you and start there.

This and the following two chapters are all about practice — things you can do — and will cover a welter of pauses of different kinds and dimensions. In this chapter we will start small, looking at how to weave short pauses into your daily life and create habits. In the next chapter, we will zoom out a bit and explore the conscious design of longer pauses that only happen from time to time. The last of these three chapters is about how we can use culture to integrate pause into the fabric of our lives over long periods. However, this isn't a series of sequential steps. It wouldn't be possible (or sensible) to try and do everything I cover here; the idea is to give you a wealth of different start points from which you can choose.

And ... action!

One of the beauties of pause is that it need not be much. A few extra seconds here or there can make all the difference. Film-maker David Keating uses a tiny pause 'the length of a breath or two' to instantly shift the mood of a film crew: 'On set, the word "action" has a certain magic, so when you delay that, even for a couple of seconds, everyone notices, not just the actors. It's not something I use as a matter of routine, but there are moments when I sense it is needed. It's powerful.'

You can have an impact on a group with nothing more than a short pause. Leaders, take note.

Sometimes a pause might not even be visible. Years ago, while on a course at Schumacher College in Devon, I met a Mexican called Jorge Kanahuati. I noticed that whenever he spoke, people listened intently. The conversation would deepen and slow, to everyone's benefit. I asked him what he was doing to create this effect. He explained that whenever he felt he had something to say, instead of acting on the impulse he would pause, and wait to see if it really needed to be said. If the idea came back, he would pause a second time. Only if the idea came back a third time would he speak up. Jorge's invisible pausing had a visible effect on the rest of us, making us better listeners and improving the quality of the conversation. Years later, I still find Jorge's story a helpful model and will, on occasion, channel my 'inner Kanahuati'.

Writer Tom Chatfield, who spends a lot of time thinking about technology, believes we underestimate the value of doing nothing at all. Acting immediately is mostly driven by the technology, not by us. Just leaving things, he says, is a powerful filter. When you come back to something later, you make a better judgement as to whether it needs doing at all. If in doubt, do nothing — far more of the time than we realise, there is no need to respond at all. 'Pause and silence are the friends of better thought,' he says.

Developing the presence of mind to pause like this is not easy. A colleague, who is a very experienced facilitator, admitted to me that she feels she has to answer questions immediately. She knows that she always gives a better answer if she gives herself a minute or two, but finds herself anxious to respond instantly. As psychologist Jon Stokes says: 'People are addicted to busy-ness, so asking them to stop is like asking people to stop taking heroin.' Trying hard is part of the problem and is likely to make things worse. Jon compares the brain to a toddler — you can't stop it doing anything, you have to distract it with something else. So, if you want to integrate pause into the everyday, you need to replace one habit (of responding immediately or constantly pushing on) with another, different habit. This is a question of practice. Practice isn't something abstract, it is embodied, so you need to engage your body as well as your mind.

Take a breath

An obvious place to start is with your breath, which connects body and mind. Since you are always breathing, the opportunity to use the breath is always at hand. When things get difficult or tense, you can simply 'take a breath' before speaking or responding. Shift your attention to your belly, softening it and letting it expand (instead of breathing from the chest), and take a gentle breath. By attending to your body for three or four seconds you can shift your mind and your mood.

This is a practice used by improvisers in the theatre. Constantly faced with the unknown and unpredictable, they get good at waiting a few seconds. Taking a breath changes you physically and mentally — it breaks the vicious circle of rush and panic. This is relevant on the business stage too. Dan Klein teaches improvisation at Stanford University, and also works with companies in the Bay Area. He says that about 40 per cent of any business audience have been told that they speak too fast when presenting. And yet, he points out, the brain can take in words faster than we can say them. The problem isn't speed per se, but failing to leave any pauses for people to digest what you say. So when speaking in public, consciously take a breath every now and then. It might feel like a yawning chasm of nothingness, but it is only a few seconds. You can always repeat a phrase, like the poet David Whyte. If your words are worth saying, then surely it is also worth allowing a few seconds for them to sink in?

This also gives you the chance to think about what to say next. The audience will thank you for giving them time to think and it will keep you and your brain nicely oxygenated.

Though we like to regard ourselves as thoughtful beings, Jon Stokes thinks we are flattering ourselves: 'Most of the time we are just reacting; we aren't doing anything that you could really call thinking.' The practice of taking a breath creates a pause between stimulus and response that gives us the chance to actually think. Over time it becomes progressively easier to interrupt the automatic habits and develop presence of mind. It doesn't get much simpler than that.

Go outside

Or does it? If breathing doesn't work for you, try walking. Integral coach Justin Wise often suggests to his clients that two or three times a day they leave their desk, go outside and walk once around the block. At first they are self-conscious. It seems a ridiculous thing to do, but Justin will insist and, to keep them to it, he asks them to make a note of when they walk. Gradually, as the judgemental thoughts recede there is space for other responses — they start to notice how they are feeling in their body (an untapped source of information), get insights or have new ideas.

After a while a walk that seemed trivial becomes indispensable and is integrated into their routine. Busy, important people report that what started as an irritating obligation becomes a necessity: as the practice deepens it requires less and less effort to keep up and consistently delivers such benefits that they wonder how they ever did without it.

Since, like breathing, walking is something you do anyway, any kind of walking provides an opportunity to develop a practice of pause. Walking and thinking are intimately linked, so walking really does provide 'pause for thought'. As you walk, it gives you the chance to metaphorically 'walk around your ideas', approaching them in different ways or looking at them from a different angle. Frederic Gros traces the importance of walking to philosophers and poets such as Nietzsche, Rousseau and Rimbaud in his delightful book *A Philosophy of Walking*. A walk, says Gros, 'is a matter of a change in rhythm: it unshackles the body's limbs along with the mind's faculties'. A short walk is simple, achievable and has immediate effects. In only five minutes you can shift your perspective and change your inner state.

Professor Dame Angela McLean is a mathematical biologist at All Souls College, Oxford. When I met with her recently to talk about creativity, she said, 'If our conversation gets stuck, we can do what I always do when I get stuck — go for a walk.' Dr Neil Randhawa, an anaesthetist in London, uses a 'walk to work' to create a collective pause with colleagues. Every now and then, he and a group of other doctors will meet at a convenient point part-way to the hospital and walk the last half-hour together. The idea is to create an 'empty space' where they can talk about whatever is on their minds, serious or silly, in a way that cannot happen once they are at work.

Paradoxical though it may sound, making the effort to walk slowly is useful if you are in a hurry. Walk fast to a meeting and you might save a few seconds, but what mental state will you arrive in? Walk at a measured pace and though you might arrive a tiny bit later, you will be in a completely different frame of mind. People around you feel the difference. This is particularly valuable if you are a leader. By slowing down your movements you can create a sense of time and space where there appears to be none. For a similar reason, people who are trained in emergency response are told not to run to a casualty because even in those extreme circumstances, it is more important to collect your thoughts than arrive a few seconds earlier.

Count to one

Often we neglect to pause because we simply forget. There is something here to learn from Zen: something which is nothing to do with the meditation or the chanting (I promised you no 'wu-wu'). In a Zen monastery, the door to the meditation hall, or 'zendo', doesn't reach all the way to the ground. There is a wooden bar across the opening at floor level which you have to step over in order to enter. This isn't because the normally meticulous Zen Buddhists are sloppy carpenters, it is deliberate. The bar forces you to pause for a moment and notice how you are entering the zendo — in what frame of mind, with what intention and so on. It gives you a moment of personal stocktaking. It acts as a speed bump — both literally and metaphorically — obliging you to pause.

An everyday version of this is to count to one before you enter a room or a meeting. Not ten, or even three, but one. That may seem insignificant, but to count to one, you have to pause. The important thing is to stop, not how long you stop for. That tiny interregnum has a similar effect to the bar across the bottom of the door: by checking you, it allows you to check in with how you are. I rather mischievously suggest this to people who are proud of how busy they are, because even they cannot claim they don't have time to count to one.

Counting can also help you hold silences, something many people find hard. If you count how long you are holding a silence for, you can see that it is never very long. A ten-second pause in a workshop — to allow people to digest an experience, or find the words to express something — is often enough, but it feels like an age. Having an objective measure of the length of a 'pregnant' pause helps you hold it for that bit longer. And after a bit of practice, it stops being uncomfortable altogether. Over time, you become able to tolerate more and longer silences. Which opens up all manner of new possibilities.

In 2008 the World Health Organisation invented a kind of speed bump for operating theatres. It is called the 'surgical safety check list'. It consists of a simple series of questions to ask before the start of an operation. Some of it is technical, but much of it isn't. For example, one of the items to check is that the team have introduced themselves to each other by name. The value of the check list lies in forcing people to pause and think. That alone creates a measurable improvement in morbidity and mortality rates. It is a more formal version of the 'gathering pause' used by singers and musicians.

A speed bump forces you to pause. A gentler option is to look for particular moments, places or routines you can use as 'triggers', so that you don't have to rely solely on memory or willpower.

The daily routine

The journey to or from work is one such trigger. Instead of regarding the commute as a nuisance, why not see it as something you can take and use? For example, you can reframe traffic jams or delays as moments to pause.[1] This doesn't necessarily imply becoming a saintlike figure, immune to the pressures of modern life. In fact, quite the opposite — you might pause in order to notice the frustration or impatience, and in so doing create a little space between you and those feelings, rather than letting them take possession of you.

You can choose to see the journey as an 'in-between' place in its own right (instead of as a waste of time). Regard it as a space not to be filled and deliberately avoid reading a book, listening to the radio or music, or checking email. See what occurs and what you notice — either about the journey, or about yourself. One friend does this when driving one of his sons to his rock-climbing class, creating an empty space where father and son can just be together. A client of mine has the practice of memorising what and who is in the carriage on the train on the way home, creating a 'cleansing' space between work and home and exercising her memory at the same time.

If you want to be specific, focus on the beginning or end of the journey. Leaving and arriving are very identifiable moments in which to create a pause that marks the boundaries of time, like a sorbet between courses at a restaurant, cleansing the palate and preparing you for what comes next.

For ten years Tom Hockaday was CEO of Isis Innovation, Oxford University's technology transfer company. He developed a very particular end-of-day routine. Before he left work, he would shut the door to his office and take five minutes to himself. In homage to jazz musician Dave Brubeck he called it 'Take Five'.

---

1 This is a fine example of using the improviser's practice of seeing everything as an offer to take and use. See my own book *Do Improvise* for more on this.

The opening those five minutes offered could be valuable in a number of ways. He might make sense of a difficulty that had occurred earlier; or remember a task that needed to be done the next day; or think about the longer-term future; or just sit quietly and daydream. One way or another, he saw it as a way to close the day, and leave work thoughts at work, rather than carrying them home with him. I am not sure if he used to play the Dave Brubeck track while he did so, but the version I have is five minutes and fifteen seconds long, so it would work pretty well if he did.

Arrivals work just as well as departures. Leadership coach Gil Dove believes that the moment you get home is a critical one. He observed that some of his clients, eager to be home, and often feeling guilty about being late, would arrive in a whirlwind. They wouldn't be conscious that they were about to enter a space where something was *already* happening. That left no room to notice what mood their partner was in, or the activity their kids were up to. This meant that though they were glad to be home, they wouldn't properly connect to their loved ones, which could lead to misunderstandings or moments of tension.

Gil's recommendation is to pause on the threshold for thirty seconds. In such a pause you can remember who it is that you are about to greet and what they mean to you. The idea is not only to jettison what you have left behind (like Tom Hockaday) but to create a sense of anticipation.

You can use any repeated activity as a trigger for a pause. Brad, a colleague in the US, would often get impatient while at the hand-dryer in the bathroom, and find himself leaving with wet hands. Realising how ridiculous this was, he consciously chose to use it as a time to pause. Doing so gave him a moment to unwind and the chance to get his hands properly dry.

Instead of using an activity as a trigger, you can also use mood. When my mind is racing and I feel overwhelmed, I use a personal mantra which kicks in as a response to anxiety. I repeat the phrase, 'There is time for everything,' over and over again. Normally I do this in my head, but if there is no one else around, I do it out loud. In making it physical it becomes more powerful. The repetitive rhythm has a calming effect, connecting me to my body and my breathing. The more I say it, the slower I go. A mantra doesn't have to be anything mystic or religious: my phrase reminds me that the sharp sense of urgency I feel is exactly that — a feeling in me, not something in the world.

The habit of writing

We know that making any activity regular makes you more likely to stick to it. So you can co-opt a regular physical practice to use as a pause. It doesn't have to be yoga or meditation. Try writing. Many writers swear by the practice of writing every day, in a semi-automatic way. Creativity guru Julia Cameron has popularised one version of this idea known as 'Morning Pages', which, unsurprisingly, you do first thing in the morning. The idea is that this allows you to 'catch yourself before your ego's defences are in place'. The timing and other specific rules she has (e.g. you must write exactly three pages) may be important if you are a creative writer, but as a way of introducing a pause, you can take a more relaxed approach.

Focus on writing as a physical activity, rather than a mental one. Write by hand (remember that?) and don't think about what you are writing. Don't even worry about writing grammatically, just keep your hand moving, as if it is disconnected from your mind (who knows, maybe it is?)

If you can't think of anything to write, just write 'I can't think of anything to write' over and over again, but don't stop. This can be strangely restful. As a bonus, it is sometimes insightful. You may find your hand has more to say than you realised. What it writes unthinkingly might turn out to be of interest.

Journalling is another way to use writing to create a reflective space. Lynda Johnson, a 'super-head' at a large comprehensive school in the north of England, told me how she had adopted the practice of journalling as a pause in her hectic day. She bought herself a notebook she liked the look and feel of, so that she was more likely to use it (as any writer knows, stationery matters). Each evening, she would spend twenty minutes or so with it. She would read as well as write, going back over previous entries and noting down her impressions of the day. She didn't do this with any particular intention in mind, or any rules for herself. This enabled her to relax and digest what had happened. Over time she also found that she was able to see patterns through the writing. She noticed when she was putting things off, or discovered themes she hadn't been aware of. So it served multiple purposes.

Daily drawing

If writing isn't your thing, draw. Get a nice sketchbook (as any artist knows, materials matter) and set yourself the task of making a drawing a day. Choose a time of day and commit an exact amount of time to it: as little as three minutes would be fine. There is no need to be artistic and no need to complete the drawing (the exercise is really about looking). Draw whatever is in front of you. You might draw an everyday object that is on your desk before you leave work. I once met a young Japanese traveller in China who drew the most mundane things. His sketchbook was full of drawings of train tickets, receipts and hotel keys. It was beautiful.

If the prospect of drawing is intimidating, doodle. Much like the automatic writing, you can let the hand be active while the mind idles. Grab a pencil and let your hand wander over the page. Sit back, watch and see what emerges. Or look the other way and doodle 'blind'. For a change, use your non-dominant hand. If you really want to take the pressure off, you could also tear out the page once you are done, screw it up and throw it away (which might become a satisfying ritual in itself).

There is a lot you could do to introduce the habit of a little pause into your everyday life. Don't let that confuse you or weigh upon you. You don't need to do all of this or any of this — it is a menu, not a prescription. Don't try too hard either. Hold the idea of pause lightly — allow yourself to entertain or explore it rather than making it another goal. If pause just becomes another task on your to-do list it won't help. You don't need to be pausing all the time. In fact, if you were, it wouldn't be a pause.

I would encourage you to aim low and be selfish. Starting small is a good way to build a habit. You don't have to make a major commitment or spend a week in silent retreat to get the benefit of pausing. You might need to do very little. As the footballer Zinedine Zidane said: 'Magic is sometimes very close to nothing at all.' It might be that all you need to do to access the magic of pause is to decide to make pause a 'thing' for yourself. Arguably, since you are here, you already have. This is called 'naming things into existence'. It works like the famous injunction, 'Don't think of an elephant'. Once you make pause a *thing*, you can't avoid thinking about it. Doing this can puncture the illusion that pushing on, keeping going or being 'always on' is good, or necessary. You can start to pay attention to whether you pause, how you pause and where you would like to pause a bit more.

Choose something easy that sounds fun, or curious, or challenging to you. It could be something from this chapter or something you invent for yourself. Be playful. Create some 'small, safe-to-fail experiments'. If it works, do more of it. If not, let it go and try something else. There is plenty more where this came from.

4
Design

For the last fifteen years I have worked on the Strategic Leadership Programme at Oxford University's Saïd Business School. Being part of the executive education faculty there has brought me into contact with a varied and fascinating set of people and ideas. Participants come from all over: Australian ambassadors, a Bulgarian telecoms executive, a Nigerian newspaper editor, the founder of a Brazilian NGO, for example. Many of them travel halfway round the world to spend a week among the dreaming spires. As part of the programme we use ideas from complexity science, psychology, history and philosophy. We work with poetry, Lego, art and music. There is a lot going on.

Yet when I ask people what they get from the experience, more often than not they say: 'Time out to think.' At first, this disappointed me. After all the care and attention we had devoted to design and delivery and all the effort they made to come, this was what they valued most?

While I was disappointed, the participants weren't. Far from it, they were enormously satisfied, consistently rating the programme 4.8 or 4.9 out of 5. I was confused. What was going on here?

When I listened to their comments more carefully, I realised that 'time out to think' is rare, in two senses. First, it is scarce. People are besieged by an unending barrage of demands. Their focus is on the immediate, their time is always under pressure and everyone wants a piece of them. Creating any time for reflection (or for themselves) is practically very difficult to do. What is true more widely is also true for this group. Leaders have no more time for themselves than anyone else.

Secondly, rare also means 'unusually good or remarkable' and that applies here too. If making time is difficult, making time to *think* is even harder. Any old time won't do. To think well involves more than the intellect. We think with our hands and our hearts, we think by moving, we think by making. We each think in different ways and we think together in conversation. The normal environment doesn't support this quality of thinking and, as a result, most of the time we are just reacting. Creating 'time out to think' takes care and attention. It is precious as well as scarce.

It took me a while to accept that this is no small thing. Our society focuses on generating 'more' of everything — more products, more growth, more money, more success — so we tend to assume that more is better. We don't invest emptiness or silence with value. So I had taken it as given that a week at Oxford would give people more 'stuff' — more models, tools, techniques and so on. I assumed that substance was superior to space. It hadn't struck me that absence — the pause in normal working life — might be the most powerful thing. And that much of the design was about creating this space. One participant, the CEO of a major charity, summed it up perfectly: 'Time out *is* time in,' he said.

This chapter is about pause on a different scale: longer, slower, deeper. The habits we explored in the last chapter tend to be rapid, short and frequent. By contrast, the pauses we will look at now have a different character — they are more subtle and less common. They are designed and considered. They shift you into a different mode (and mood). On the one hand they are a relief and a release from the everyday, yet they also have great intensity. They reveal new information, often making visible what matters most. They enable you to make discoveries and take decisions you would never reach in the thick of everyday life.

This kind of pause doesn't only happen on a programme like the one at Oxford. Bill Gates invented his own. Once every two years he would commit to a 'Think Week'. He would retreat to a remote spot with a carefully chosen pile of books and papers, disconnect from the everyday, immerse himself in reading and think about the big issues. This enabled him to see patterns, get insights and reach conclusions that couldn't have occurred to him in the office. My colleague Tracey Camilleri says that in such a week 'you are able to think long thoughts'. From those 'long thoughts' significant changes in Microsoft's strategy would result.

Think Weeks are becoming common with tech leaders. Maybe people always copy whatever Bill Gates does, but I think there is more to it than that. The tech leaders' world is dominated by the fast and the new, so they are well placed to see that every now and then you need to work, consciously and deliberately, at a different rhythm.

This isn't something that only applies to the tech industry. Whoever you are, taking 'time out to think' matters — professionally and personally. The knee-jerk response to just work harder won't help: that is part of the problem. Rather than knuckling down or pushing on, you need to step back. As Einstein famously said, 'No problem can be solved from the same level of consciousness that created it.' In a pause like a Reading Weekend, or a Think Week, you access a different kind of consciousness, which might reveal you are looking at the wrong problem, or looking in the wrong way. You might become aware of your own assumptions and biases. Every once in a while, it is worth doing something to change your mind.

These larger pauses are too infrequent to be driven by habit. And they don't happen automatically. It is easy to keep stalling. The very idea of such pauses runs counter to the prevailing culture, where 'time out' is generally regarded as time off, rather than 'time in'.

For example, the other day I mentioned I was writing a book about pause to a couple I had just met. Without missing a beat, one of them immediately said: 'But there is always a cost to pausing.' She was genuinely puzzled by the idea that pause was worth thinking (or writing) about. She was resistant to it, even slightly indignant. There was an awkward silence. A pause, in fact. After a minute or more her husband added: 'Perhaps ... but there is always a cost to not pausing as well.'

This is a perfect illustration of the dilemma we are caught in. We assume that pausing is going to cost us — either now or in the future. The feeling is immediate, instinctive and compelling. It is how we have been trained to think. It takes a little reflection to recognise the cost of not pausing. To see the value of pause, you first have to pause. We are easily caught in a never-ending loop.

To break that loop and create deeper, longer pauses takes conscious effort. The first thing to do is recognise the need; to acknowledge that there is a value in time out that you cannot get any other way. You need to be able to create a pause for yourself, or perhaps — since it starts as an attitude or a belief — it would be more accurate to say, *in* yourself. For me, it helps to think that: 'Busy is the new lazy'. Busy keeps things the same; hectic, but unchanging. It is a kind of avoidance, and that's lazy.

Action vs Activity

Improv actors have some useful language here. They distinguish between 'action' and 'activity'. Action is what they need to create a story. It changes things — for the characters they are playing and for the audience. A simple line like 'It was me' or 'I'm pregnant' is action because it changes our understanding. This is different from 'activity'. Activity is stuff happening. Activity may be busy or fast — one character chasing after another — but it doesn't make a difference to the story. The difference is important. You can't create a story or engage an audience with activity.

In these terms, busy-ness is activity. If you want action, i.e. if you want to do something that is going to make a difference, you need to be able to interrupt those patterns of activity, which means finding a way to pause. Creating an interregnum is thus not a sign of failure or breakdown, as we often assume it to be, but a sign of effectiveness. As psychologist and philosopher William James said: 'Eagerness, breathlessness and anxiety are not signs of strength, they are signs of weakness and bad co-ordination.'

So make pausing a priority. Promise yourself that you will regularly carve out a proper space where you are not consumed by the need to complete tasks, and can pay attention to different things. Take responsibility for creating this and commit to it. Careful design can help (we will get to that in a moment) but you need to start with the conviction that this matters.

You will need conviction because you will have to confront doubts and scepticism — your own, as well as other people's. Pausing is uncomfortable and unpopular. It is likely you will be criticised — explicitly, or implicitly. The moral high ground belongs to those who get on with things, not those that 'delay'. You will find plenty of reasons in your mind why 'now is not the time'. Expect all this and pause anyway. Be willing to act on the basis of feeling, not reasons. Be prepared to pause without being sure what it will bring you. There is power in starting before you are ready. Or, to put the same thing another way, if you wait until you are completely ready, you will never start.

Consider Chris Riley, who I mentioned at the beginning of this book. Chris came all the way from Oregon to attend a Reading Weekend in Spain. He liked it so much that he wanted to do it every year: but only afterwards. The first time, it was a struggle. He was unsure of why he had come or what it would bring. While he was in it, he felt uneasy and was honest enough to admit that to himself at the time and to me afterwards. Nonetheless, something brought him all that way. He was willing to act on a hunch. As a result, he put it in the diary, booked flights and made a commitment to me, a friend as well as the organiser, so that he *had* to come.

It need not take long and it need not be frequent. For Chris Riley it was three days in a year. For Bill Gates it was one week in a hundred. Participants in Oxford often say, 'This has been an amazing week' — after only two days. Not all time is created equal. Let yourself go fully into a pause and you find yourself plunged into 'other kinds of time'. You don't get *more* time, but you can get more *from* the time you have.

Pause well, and it is extraordinary what can happen in a short space of time. As another participant on the Reading Weekend put it: 'Time is different here: baggy, generous: ambling, then dashing at the pace of light and landscape.' This is hard to appreciate from the outside, and that contributes to the scepticism. Apply the normal yardstick and you miscalculate. I had one client who was adamant that three days was nowhere near long enough for his leadership-team retreat. He had to travel a long way and wanted to make sure it was worth it — an understandable but unhelpful sentiment. And yet, by the third day he was perfectly ready to leave. We had done more than he thought possible and he acknowledged that any longer would have been too much.

Don't underestimate the value of even short periods. If a Think Week feels impossible, try a day. Don't skip it altogether just because you don't have a week. Don't let the ambition to do something big stop you doing something small. Johnnie Moore, founder of 'Unhurried Conversations', has adopted the practice of what he calls 'scheduled rambles'. Every month or so, he spends an hour or two in conversation, with no particular goal, with someone he finds interesting (often on Skype). It is an easy, zero-cost way to design a different kind of time into your schedule. He finds that even this short period is regenerative.

Pause is not linear

Just as a few seconds changes the entire mood on a film set, a few days can shift, or anchor, a whole year. A few hours can change your week. We overestimate how long a pause needs to be and underestimate how long its effects will last. A parent who came to 'The Creative Tapas Experience' — a weekend event I ran, focused on making — told me: 'Eighteen months later, those two days are still nourishing our family.' A short time can be a long time.

This is because a pause allows you to sink into things. Your perception is clear and the experience is vivid. It is memorable and meaningful. In the improviser's language, this is action. It is a striking contrast to the blur of activity we experience when rushing around with an unending to-do list. It is the yeast to the everyday dough. You need both to make bread.

This is where good design comes into play. It is design that makes the time people spend on the leadership programme at Oxford so powerful. When done well it can be 'close to nothing', but creating an 'empty' space takes a lot of care and attention. This means thinking like an artist and paying attention to the 'negative space' which lies in between and around the main elements. You need to give importance to meals, journeys and coffee breaks as well as lectures, activities and tasks. With one of my clients, the most important ideas always occur in the breaks, so we make them more frequent. The rhythm and cadence of the whole is shaped by the relationship between sessions and spaces. Content plays a role, but it is not the most important thing.

I spend much of my time designing different kinds of events and retreats, for all sorts of different groups: corporate and professional teams, groups, families and individuals. The idea you can design emptiness might sound strange, but a pause needs to be contained, and you can design the container.

Stay open

Start with the objective: don't have one. Or if you must, make it open and broad. I prefer intentions to objectives (or goals). It feels more open. If you tightly define what you want, and succeed, all you get is exactly what you expected. You are limited by your own goal. Which is a waste. This is a big change from business as normal, where we define the outcomes we want, precisely, in advance. That makes sense if you are focused on a task, but a pause is not a task. You need to be tight about some things (who comes, leaving normal work in the office) but open to what emerges.

On the Reading Retreats we ask people to bring questions that are alive for them, not problems to solve. We allow things to unfold from there, which means the questions themselves can change, or new ones appear. Ideas come from unlikely sources. As a result, without really trying, we cover more ground and make more connections than we could possibly anticipate. And the learning is different for everyone. I know we will surprise ourselves and I am highly confident that we will solve some problems. Just don't ask me which ones they will be in advance. Having an open intention, not a specific goal, is what makes this possible.

The power of place

For a retreat-like pause, place is the single most important choice you make. The quickest, most powerful way to create a mental shift is via contact with nature and beauty. This is crashingly obvious but its importance cannot be overstated. Too often we surrender to the practical difficulties involved: 'It will take too long to get there' or 'How will it look?' Yet we are more profoundly affected by our immediate environment than by anything else. To create an effective pause, you should use the power of place.

Nature and beauty give perspective, contrast and inspiration. When we are immersed in nature we reconnect with our natural selves. Not all time is created equal. An hour in a good place is worth more than a day in an average place. There is a reason that the Do Lectures happen on a farm in Wales, or the Burning Man Festival is held in the desert.

This doesn't mean you necessarily have to be in a rural or remote environment. At Oxford we consciously use the beauty and history of the city itself. One colleague jokingly refers to it as the 'medieval theme park', but the dreaming spires do just what it says on the tin — they encourage people to dream and they inspire.

The cloistered charms of Oxford are obvious, but even in the busiest city there are plenty of quiet, thought-provoking spots. You just have to seek them out. Imagine you are in London. You could go down to the Thames foreshore at Rotherhithe. The smell of mud and the calling of gulls makes you feel as if you have left the city behind. The shift in perspective and rhythm is palpable. Give people something to contemplate here and they will come up with radically different responses than they would in the office.

There's history there too — the pub next door is called the Mayflower. It was from here that the original *Mayflower* set sail for Plymouth, before heading west to America. Opposite the pub is the Rotherhithe Picture Library. Housed in another ancient building, with massive oak beams, it is a collection of images and photographs you couldn't possibly find online, chaotically disorganised in musty old scrapbooks. Seeing different images helps you see things differently. Spend an hour there and you will feel like you have been away for months. You might be offered a cup of tea by the locals who work there as volunteers and find yourself in conversation with someone who lives at a different rhythm from you.

All of this is in central London, no more than half an hour's walk along the river from the Shard or the City. But whoever thinks to go there? I had known the area for over thirty years before I discovered all this, simply because I wasn't looking. Good places to create a pause, like the Rotherhithe foreshore, are everywhere, if you look for them. The parks, gardens, squares, cathedrals, canals and rooftops of any city are at your disposal. Use them.

Spaces are defined by their boundaries. As well as the physical boundary, that also means making conscious choices about connectivity. Be clear, realistic and firm about this — even if you are only designing something for yourself. For a pause to do its work, you need a degree of disconnection from the everyday and you must signal this to other people, so they understand you are not available for business as usual. That is why Bill Gates cuts himself off from normal communication for his Think Weeks.

This isn't trivial, so think about it carefully. On a retreat, do you ask people to surrender their phones altogether? Or is that just going to be a source of tension? Do you use humour, or fines, or forfeits for transgressions? Is there a particular time of day you ring-fence for connection? Innocent (the smoothie company) held a festival in the countryside south of London which ran on solar energy called 'Innocent Unplugged'. They encouraged people to leave their phones behind. As far as I could see there was no enforcement but it quickly became the norm that phones stayed in the campsite.

There is no single answer here, it is always going to depend on context, but as they say in the countryside,

'Good fences make good neighbours.' If you want to get the benefit of a pause you need to think about how you are going to fence it off. One simple way to do that is to choose a place where there isn't much coverage, something I imagine Innocent took into account when selecting their location. Many of the pauses I design are run at locations in rural Spain where there is little mobile phone coverage and rickety Wi-Fi. At the end of one 'Parenthesis' — a time out for professionals — a participant from the US said: 'The Wi-Fi here is crap. [pause] Make sure you keep it that way.'

Create some space

The fetish that exists around productivity means that to create an empty space you sometimes need a little sleight of hand and a plausible cover story. To satisfy onlookers, overseers or sceptical participants you should be able to present a programme of activity that looks detailed and sounds respectable, but don't take it too literally. The aim is to create some space, not a packed timetable.

Earlier this year I helped design a CEO summit for a global company. This included an empty, unscheduled day at the end. There was enormous pressure to fill this, in order to 'make the most of our time together', but the leader resisted. As it happened, the 'empty' day turned out to be vital. It provided a space to process, digest and make sense of the previous days. Without it, the event would not have been as successful as it was. Defending the boundaries of empty space is important and it takes courage. You have to have the heart for it.

Instead of filling the time as if it were the agenda for a meeting, think about what will create the mood or energy you are looking for. What kind of activity or materials will help? For a Think Week you could choose a theme and select reading based on that, but there are many other possibilities, depending on the kind of pause you want to create for yourself or others.

The Creative Tapas Experience was designed to get people out of their everyday world through an experience of making. It was deliberately playful, so rather than books or articles there was a wealth of materials to make things with including paper, cardboard, string, tape, Plasticine, clay, rope, cloth, costumes, chicken wire, wood, brick, stone and old car tyres. Engaging the hand is one way to pause the mind. The materials and the activities were designed to support that.

As well as materials, think about the rules you choose to govern your pause. A little structure is needed, or people will simply do what they normally do. You don't need much. For the Creative Tapas Experience we didn't assign people to teams, give them a brief, or allocate working space or materials. They were free to choose all that for themselves. We had only three guidelines:

1. *No solo creations*

2. *Nothing you make to last longer than seven minutes*

3. *Be ready at 9pm*

This was enough structure to mobilise sixty people over twenty-four hours to make nearly thirty different creations, including sculptures, films, performances and a football tournament (that lasted only seven minutes). Empty space did the rest.

Similarly, the Reading Weekend has only two rules. We choose many different books, but there is only one copy of each. So the first rule is: 'One book at a time'.

You can keep a book for as long (or as short) as you like, but you can only have one at a time from the book table. The rest have to stay there. The second rule is: 'Read between meals, talk over meals'. This is all you need to run the whole weekend.

Establish a pattern of pauses

The beauty of these longer pauses is how much they give you. A carefully designed pause every once in a while can last you a long time. Which is also a conundrum. Since they happen infrequently, how do you establish a pattern that ensures you don't forget or skip them?

One way to do this is to set aside a 'time budget' for them. One week a year? A long weekend every quarter? An afternoon once a month? Whatever it is, plan it in and commit to spending it. You could work with the seasons. When are there natural lulls that you could take advantage of? In Spain, things inevitably quieten down in the summer, so I could use that. For years my business partner, Gary, and I found that in December no one was available for the improv workshops that were our business. If they weren't busy finishing things before the end of the year, they were out to lunch. So we decided to work with that, not against it. Even if someone asked us to do something in December, we would say no. We used that pause in all sorts of different ways: to develop new stuff, review the past year, spend time chatting, or concentrate on family. Consciously deciding this felt very different from being idle.

You can use the seasons as a metaphor too. The times for tilling, sowing and harvesting feel very different. They have a different energy. Use that. When are you harvesting and when is it appropriate to let things lie fallow? Which times are spring, summer, autumn or winter in your work, irrespective of the date on the calendar. This will give you a sense of where you might want to put some pause and can release you from feeling you have to push on with everything, all the time.

How about using your birthday as a trigger? This is a landmark you are unlikely to forget, so why not take advantage of it to instigate an annual pause? Take the day off, or establish a practise you do on that day; reviewing the past year or setting goals for the year to come. If that feels too much like hard work on your *actual* birthday you could give yourself an 'official' birthday like the Queen of England, and build your annual pause around that. That way you can choose a time of year that is appropriate for you. I might choose April Fool's Day, for example.

Beyond the fleeting pauses that punctuate the daily ebb and flow, lie slower pauses that go deeper and last longer. These are pauses of a different character. They are not a substitute for the smaller pauses, nor an improvement on them, but a complement, an altogether different place to start that might suit you. This kind of pause is a matter of design, not habit.

When you choose to go to an event like the Do Lectures, attend a programme at Schumacher College or go along to an 'Unhurried Conversation', you are making conscious choices. When does it suit you to go? How long for? What kind of event, people, place? So even when you use a ready-made pause there are still design choices involved. But, like Bill Gates, you can choose to make your own (solo or with others).

If so, by all means build on others' ideas but don't just copy someone else: take the chance to craft it in a way that suits you. Play around and have some fun. It isn't possible to be formulaic anyway, because designing a fruitful pause requires some subtlety and little bit of paradox:

— *Plan it, but stay open*

— *Set an intention not a goal*

— *Resist the temptation to narrowly define success in advance*

— *Take advantage of the power of place*

— *Set boundaries and stick to them*

— *Use whatever materials and activities suit your purpose*

— *Create some simple rules and allow improvisation*

Designing a pause is a creative process, so take this as a series of start points to stimulate your thinking, not a comprehensive check list.

Beyond the particulars of what you might design, there is an important shift of power here. By designing pauses for yourself, you have a hand in crafting how you experience time. This weakens the sense that your life is governed by an external, mechanical beat, set by someone else (or by a device) and allows you to move at a rhythm that is more your own.

5
Culture

In Arenas de San Pedro in central Spain, where I live, the olive harvest happens at the beginning of December. Or at the end of November. It isn't possible to be exact because when it is depends upon how the crop is ripening, which in turn is a result of the kind of autumn weather we have had. Nature doesn't fix dates in the diary.

Harvesting olives is work, but not as most of us know it. It is a physical job, grounded in a physical place that produces a physical result — in our case about 90 litres of extra virgin olive oil. The weather is always pleasant during harvest, not because the climate in this part of Spain is so benign, but because water spoils the crop, so if there is any damp or rain, it has to wait.

It doesn't take much effort or skill. You lay out nets under the trees and, using long wooden poles, strike the branches so the olives fall into the nets. You collect and sieve them to get rid of the twigs and leaves, and pour them into sacks. This isn't complicated, but it is absorbing. Since our olive grove is on a slope you have to solve the puzzle of how to rig the nets to catch the olives that fly off down the hill. Sometimes, you have to climb a tree to reach the far-flung branches where, inevitably, most of the fruit seems to be found. Despite the risk to limbs — both your own and the tree's — it is easy to get obsessed with reaching the last few olives.

At the end of the day, you join the chaotic throng of locals that passes for a queue in these parts, outside the *almazara* (cooperative press), to deliver the fruits of your day's work and chew the fat. You may have to wait for hours, but no one tries to speed it up or make it more efficient. It is a chance to see people you haven't seen for months and hear their news; or to meet new people and listen to their stories. The wait creates connections within the community, something nobody intended or designed, but which works anyway. There is no possible way to hurry any of this. Whatever you do, it takes the time it takes. The only hacks around here are made with axes.

The olive harvest may not be precise, but it is a regular pattern. It is the beginning of the end of the year and ushers in the Christmas season, so it always feels a little festive. For my neighbour Vicente, who works the land all year round (he has cherries, figs and chestnuts as well as olives), it is simply what he does, but for me it provides a welcome winter pause. Working with the irregular rhythms of nature, outdoors, in a beautiful spot, with friends and family is delightful and therapeutic in equal measure. Our olive grove may be only a few kilometres from my desk, but it is a world away from sitting at the computer.

As well as being a matter of habit, or design, you can draw on culture to create some pauses in your life. You can weave them into the fabric of the way you live and work, so that you don't even think about it. Pause can become part of what you do and who you are.

The simplest way to do this is to change where you spend

your time. The science-fiction writer William Gibson once said: 'The future is already here, it is just not evenly distributed.' The implication is that some places are ahead of others. However, if the future is unevenly distributed, then, by implication, so is the past. You could also say: 'The past is still here, it is just unevenly distributed.' The past isn't necessarily retrograde, it is a place where the latest technology hasn't been adopted yet and being up to date isn't regarded as important. As a result, older, more measured rhythms continue to exist, people aren't in so much of a hurry and the here and now is appreciated more for itself than as a means to get somewhere else. If, in that sense, the past is still here somewhere, you can use that to your advantage.

Time does not flow equally in all places. How it feels depends upon where you are and the culture you connect to or immerse yourself in. This brings a whole new meaning to the phrase 'time zone': it isn't about the hour on the clock, but about how you *experience* time in a certain place. If you move house, you can shift from one 'time zone' to another, even in the space of a few miles. That is what happened for me when I swapped Europe's third largest city for an area known as 'Deep Spain'. Arenas de San Pedro is close enough for me to hop in the car, drive to Madrid, watch a game of football and drive home again. Nonetheless, it is a different world.

People here live at their own pace. They rarely say anything new; talk is not about relaying information, it is a way of seeing others and being with them. Conversations are conventional; often repetitive, almost ritual. If these were the only conversations I had it would suffocate me, but they act as a counterweight to overstimulation and excess novelty.

For example, one day earlier this year I was walking around the reservoir at the foot of our hill with a friend from Sweden. It was a clear winter morning, the air was like glass and the snow-capped peaks of the Sierra de Gredos were reflected in the still water. I stopped to greet 'Old Boni' who, like us, was on his morning walk, albeit at a gentler pace. He gestured up to the mountains with his stick: 'Isn't this the most beautiful place in the world,' he said. It wasn't a question. I translated for my friend and added: 'Of course, he's never been anywhere else.' Nonetheless here he was, taking it all in, as if he were seeing it for the first time.

Old culture

Both the landscape itself, and how people like Boni respond to it, affect me. Over time, I find that instead of getting bored and looking for new stimulation, my capacity for appreciating what I have deepens. Arenas may be the past, but it doesn't feel backward: it feels human, real and meaningful. From here, technology, so often part of the problem, works in my favour. It allows me to connect to the fast-moving world when I choose, but at any moment, all I have to do is lift my head and I can take in the vast, timeless beauty of the sierra. Access to a direct, visceral experience of pause is on hand all the time — 24/7 as they might say in faster places: mountains during the day; stunning starscapes, untainted by light pollution, at night.

It was serendipity that brought me here. Others make more conscious choices to shift the rhythm of their life by connecting to a different culture. Travel writer Pico Iyer chose to leave his 'dream job' and an apartment on Park Avenue in New York City to live in a single room in the backstreets of Kyoto, Japan. 'I was racing around so much I could never catch up with my life.' So he decided to move to a place 'where people had been sitting still for eight hundred years'. He acknowledges the cost involved: 'It is not ideal for job advancement, cultural excitement or social diversion.' But what he gets in exchange is more important to him: 'Sometimes making a living and making a life point in opposite directions.'

Of course, just because you live somewhere doesn't mean you have to stay there all the time. Like me, Pico Iyer still travels: trains, planes and automobiles can take you back to places as well as away from them. I recently spent a week in Silicon Valley, at the NASA Ames Research Center in Mountain View. I was working with Singularity University — an organisation focused on cutting-edge technology and its implications. I was there with a group of technical experts — astrobiologists, cyber-ecologists and natural language programmers — talking about the latest advances in artificial intelligence, genetics and space exploration. Yet, modern aviation being what it is, only twenty hours after leaving San Francisco, I was back home, nestling in the lee of the Sierra de Gredos, among people who neither know nor care about unicorns or exponential change, for whom 'start up' is what you need your chainsaw to do.

In Arenas de San Pedro it is hard to get stressed or anxious, even if you wanted to. There might be other difficulties (a hail storm might destroy the cherry crop) but relentless time pressure isn't one of them. A place like this is a resource, as well as somewhere to live. It invites me to pause and helps me to get back to a tempo I choose, not one that is chosen for me.

By contrast Silicon Valley, or any metropolitan area, abounds with new ideas and possibilities. The people there are busy inventing the future. Which is cool. But the very same qualities that make it 'cutting edge' come at a cost. The ceaseless, highly competitive focus on what comes next brings anxiety, pressure and stress.

The point is not that one is better than the other. They are different. And just as it would be hard to be at the forefront of technology from Arenas de San Pedro, it is hard to make pause a significant part of your life if you only ever spend time in major cities. Whether 'today is the slowest day of the rest of your life' depends on where you spend the rest of those days. What interests me is how you can use different places to fulfil your needs. If the past is still here, simply by moving, you can have direct access to a deep source of pause.

You don't have to move permanently. You can choose how and where to place yourself. Chris Riley's annual visit to the Reading Weekend became something of a pilgrimage. From the outset he was well aware of the power of an annual event, integrated into his calendar, allowing him to extend its effect: anticipation in advance, synthesis afterwards. He is one of a number of people who regularly visit and only part of the reason they come is to see me. None of them plan to move here. They come in order to reconnect to a place that mediates a pause for them. Some of them have very particular spots they return to. For one, it is a rock by the River Pelayos — quite literally, a touchstone. Where might you find yours?

The irony is, slow places work fast. The old house in Avila where we hold the Reading Weekends, with its 1.5-meter-thick granite walls, envelops you, and the agitation of city life quickly evaporates. In its place a sense of stillness seeps into you. I defy anyone to spend even a single day at a place like La Serna and not feel a significant change in their inner state. Much as you are the company you keep, the places you inhabit, inhabit you. If you want to pause, changing where you spend time is one of the simplest, most immediate and most powerful ways of doing so. It draws on a deep well of culture.

New cultures

Tapping into an older, slower culture is one possibility. Creating new culture is another. Take the Burning Man Festival, for example. What began as a small spontaneous gathering on Baker Beach, just below the Golden Gate Bridge, on the summer solstice in 1986 has become an extraordinary experiment on a massive scale.

Black Rock City, 'a vibrant participatory metropolis' (with its own airport), is a temporary home to over seventy thousand 'burners'. The City rises up out of nothing, in the middle of nowhere, for a few days every year in the desert in Nevada. It is not one thing, but many; a vast creative array of experiments and experiences of every imaginable (and unimaginable) kind. It is vibrant, energetic and extreme, but it isn't just about sex and drugs and rock and roll. For example, it has a strong intellectual strand. Serious thinkers go there and the talks and debates heard at Burning Man reflect that.

This is pause as a suspension of the status quo, designed to try things out, not slow them down. It is an enormous, joyful experiment in radical inclusion, self-reliance and self-expression where the normal rules of society are suspended.

For those who attend it has real lasting power, creating an opportunity to escape William Blake's 'mind-forged manacles', and leaving a 'positive hangover'. Some 'burners' give themselves a different name for the duration of the festival — quite literally pausing who they normally are and experimenting with being somebody else.

The Burning Man is a liminal or transitional space that allows people to push boundaries and try things out in a way that isn't normally possible. It is intentional and purposive. Its aim is: 'To generate society that connects each individual to his or her creative powers, to participation in the community, to the larger realm of civic life and to the even greater world of nature that exists beyond society.'

This matters. For people who go, there is something psychologically healthy about getting out of your normal physical and mental routines. For society at large, including those who aren't even aware of it, opening up such a vast and creative liminal space is still of value. As we have seen in so many other contexts, if you aren't able to pause to consider or explore alternatives, it is extremely difficult to change direction.

The weekly pause

The idea of a regular pause woven into the social fabric of life is an old one. Based on an original idea by god, many religious traditions include the idea of a day of rest. They integrate this into the weekly rhythm, which makes it easy to observe. You don't have to think about it, the pause that the sabbath brings is simply there for you. It is ordained. Others know not to bother you.

Like many old traditions it has a connection to nature. I discovered this at a Jewish wedding on the outskirts of Madrid. The religious service couldn't take place until the Sabbath was over and that meant waiting for the first star to come out. So a couple of hundred smartly dressed people stood staring into the sky, trying to distinguish passing planes and satellites from actual stars, in order for the couple to make their vows.

You can adopt or adapt a sabbath for yourself, even if you aren't religious.[2] I had a close friend at university who was Jewish. I would often go round to visit her on a Saturday morning, because I knew she would be having tea in her room, listening to music and chatting with friends. Gradually, it became an informal part of my weekly rhythm too.

When the final exams came, I was struggling. I tried to work all the time, which meant I got the worst of both worlds — I studied badly and never got a proper break. I was envious of my friend, who had a clear pattern she didn't have to think about. So I decided to copy her. I realised I was free to borrow that element of the Jewish tradition for myself and built in a regular non-study day, from sunset on Friday to sunset on Saturday. Knowing it was coming would help me keep working all week; an example of the 'forward anchor' I mentioned in Chapter Two. Once it arrived, I enjoyed a guilt-free day off. No more agonising about whether I should be studying or not. It was, as it were, god-given.

These days many people have applied the idea of the sabbath to technology: for example, 'screen-free Saturdays'. Like a regular sabbath this is embedded in a weekly routine, giving you a structure of pause. 'Digital detoxes' are in the same vein, though normally they are longer and less frequent. People often use major holidays as a trigger, just as they do for a dietary detox.

What kind of a sabbath would serve you? It could be related to technology, or it could be traditional — like

---

2 See *Religion for Atheists* by Alain de Botton. He argues, convincingly in my view, that whatever you believe, there is plenty of wisdom woven into religions.

Sunday lunch. My sister has made a traditional roast lunch on Sundays part of her family culture and not just because they like cooking and food. It is a deliberate anchor point in the week for the whole family. It is a time to slow down and be together.

The sobremesa

In Spain, building a pause around a meal is a fundamental part of the culture. They believe in savouring your food, and that takes time. In the past, people would take to their beds for a solid couple of hours known as 'the pyjama and chamber pot siesta'.[3] Modern life doesn't allow for this, but even so, things do stand still for a while at lunchtime. I feel sorry for tourists, who often don't realise that between 2pm and 5pm, outside the biggest cities and the coastal resorts, there won't be anything open. The locals are lunching, slowly, and then enjoying either a *siesta* or the *sobremesa*. *Sobremesa* is the time spent at table after the meal is finished, with coffee or drinks, talking or joking. There will be some of this even with a group of colleagues eating a work-day lunch in Madrid. This is a world away from grabbing a sandwich at your computer. Why not take time for lunch? You might not live in Spain like I do, but you can be a bit Spanish, just as I was a bit Jewish at university.

---

3 There are other kinds of siesta too. My favourite is the 'Bishop's siesta', which takes place mid-morning. I think this should be reinstated, as a matter of urgency.

The year-long pause

The 'sabbatical year' is a longer version of the sabbath. It is an established feature of academic culture but is starting to be seen in other walks of life. A famous example is the New York designer Stefan Sagmeister, who every few years takes a whole year off. In that time he resolutely takes no work from clients (he even turned down a brief from Barack Obama's campaign during one sabbatical).

He began it 'to fight routine and boredom' and at first had fears that the clients would not come back after the sabbatical was over. In fact, the opposite happened. He claims it is both the best creative idea and the best business idea he has ever had. It is good for creativity, because it allows him to travel, think and discover. Disconnecting from the constraints of client work gives him freedom. He can explore new ideas and material without any particular brief or need in mind. It is a good business idea because those creative seeds change the trajectory of the studio. The new ideas and thinking that the break creates become the engine of business growth when he returns. It is also highly visible and says a lot about who he is, which creates anticipation and adds to his renown.

A sabbatical need not be so dramatic. Iain McIntosh, a finance director and former McKinsey consultant, has evolved a very different approach, almost by accident. He simply takes a pause between jobs, repeatedly. He uses his understanding of a company's time lines — like financial years and reporting periods — to engineer a break for himself, carefully managing the expectations of future employers as he does so. Sometimes he manages a month or two, occasionally as long as six months. Over the course of a career, it adds up. He has managed to create a lot of pauses throughout his life, almost imperceptibly.

Since the financial world is more conservative than the world of design, this suits him much better.

His reasons for taking time out are also more personal than Sagmeister's. He sees these breaks as a way to 'pick up on the parts of life that are neglected when I am working hard'. As well as redressing an imbalance it gives him 'a bit of objectivity on work and life'. It allows him space to think about bigger questions (like 'Am I in the right line of work?') and do 'some fun stuff'. He travels, spends time supporting and helping his family, meets with people he wouldn't normally see and learns new skills. These breaks also allow him to attend to what he describes as 'the siren call of the big books'.

Sabbaticals can play many different roles and have very different characters. I left a plum job at a top London advertising agency to go travelling for a year. That was in 1990. I still haven't made it back. Along the way I discovered a new country, culture and language, met my wife and found a completely different way to make a living. It morphed into a whole new life. Sometimes the pause turns out to be more significant than what it interrupts.

Give it a name

Language helps create culture. We all know what a 'sabbath' is. When Bill Gates calls his retreats Think Weeks he gives them substance and raises their status. The name reminds him why he is doing it. It acts as a signal to other people — this is not time off, it's a 'think week'. Names make things sticky. Having a label like 'Screen Free Saturdays' is both explanatory and memorable. It makes you more likely to do it. Naming things also gives you a chance to be playful and have fun. 'Take Five' for example.

You can borrow words and ideas that support your pauses from other cultures. Because I live in Spain, I steal a lot from the Spanish, who have a lot of phrases related to pause and rest — such as *siesta* and *sobremesa*. When the Spanish want to pause to consider something overnight they say they are going to 'consult with their pillow'. The image is more vivid and stickier than the English 'sleep on it'. Consider who you could borrow language from to help you name and give life to your own pauses.

Do paws

If you want just one single thing to do to compel you to build a culture of pause into your life there is a simple way to do it. Get a dog. As the slogan goes, 'A dog is for life, not just for Christmas', so this is not something to take lightly. But that's the point. It is a double commitment — to the dog and to pausing.

Dogs need to be walked. Depending on the kind of dog, they might need walking a lot or a little, but every dog needs to be walked, every day. Moreover, dogs don't just need to go for a walk, they *love* to go for a walk. At the first sniff of a walk they become deliriously, tail-waggingly happy.

This will be the highlight of your dog's day, and for you it will be a pause.

It will give you the chance to disconnect from whatever you are doing or thinking, go outside, ruminate, reflect or daydream. As you walk your dog, your dog walks you. Your focus shifts to another living creature, so you are taken out of yourself. It is likely that some of the dog's mood will rub off on you, so it will cheer you up. The beauty of this is that it never stops. You can never tick it off your to-do list. You will have to do it again. And again. And again, for as long as you have the dog. It becomes an integral part of your day, every day.

This has an additional and important benefit. Dr Mike Evans, a specialist in preventative medicine, says that the single best thing you can do for your health is to walk for half an hour a day. This has an effect across a broad range of conditions including dementia, diabetes and depression. In longitudinal studies (of Harvard alumni) it even reduces the likelihood of death. You don't need a dog for this, but a dog will keep you to it.

I could have dedicated my last book, *Do Improvise*, to our dog. When I am writing, I get stuck in the mental world. There is always more to do, so I feel I have to keep pushing on. I know a short walk is the best kind of pause to break a creative block but I find it hard to act upon. Cosmo, who was mostly labrador, was always pining for a walk, which helped me get out the door. The walks I took with him got me unstuck many times. Now he is no longer with us, I have to do that for myself.

For pause to become a part of your life it helps to connect to something outside yourself. Borrowing from different cultures or subcultures is a powerful way to do that. You can draw on the language and customs of people, places or contexts that work at a different rhythm to your own, creating both the opportunity and the obligation to pause. This can tip you into a different pattern where pause no longer requires effort, but comes with the territory. Which is a peaceful place to be.

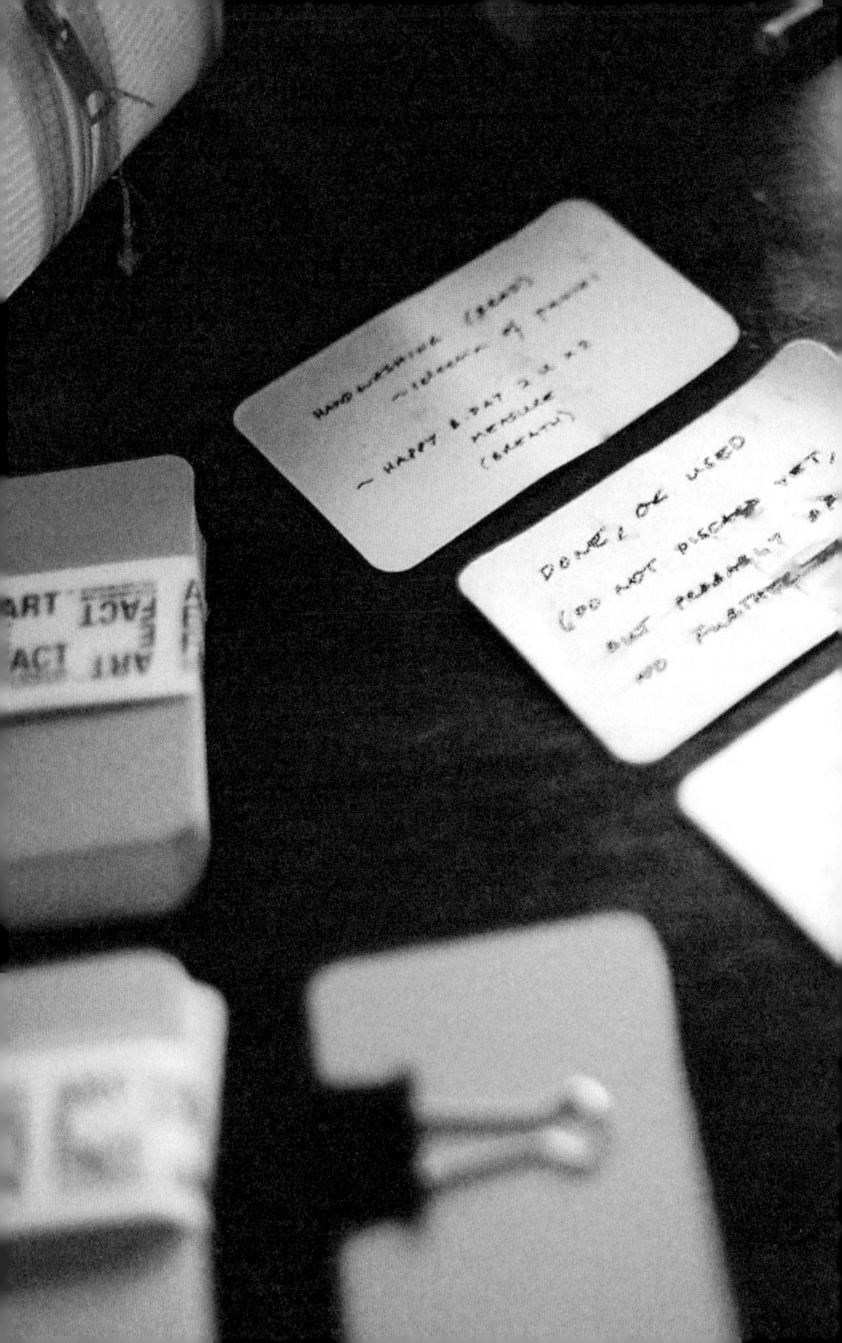
ART FACT
DONE OR USED

6
Tools

How can you put these ideas into action? Where should you start? There is a lot to choose from — everything from planning a year off to counting to one before you enter a room. We often assume that breaking things down into small pieces helps to make things manageable, so that must be the way to start. That isn't necessary here. The different levels of practice we have explored in the previous three chapters — of habits, design and culture — each have a different character, but they are not a sequence of steps.

The only authority here is you. No one else can tell you what you want or need because only you know how you feel. So let's start with that. Clearly the idea of 'pause' holds some allure for you or you wouldn't be reading this at all. Ask yourself, what is that? What drew you to this book? Why are you reading it *now*? Do you want to feel less frantic? Have more new ideas? Connect better with the people you love? Meet entirely new people? Make better decisions? Appreciate what you already have? You might just be curious about what would happen if you opened up some space.

Take a moment to notice what your interest is here: as the essayist William Hazlitt said, 'Whatever interests is interesting'. What is your felt sense of what you want to create for yourself? Take a moment to reflect on that. Specific ideas may have already caught your attention as you were reading. If so, then note what they are. If not, ask yourself what you might want to work on, or if that sounds too serious, what you might want to play around with. Don't grasp at a quick, definitive answer, just let yourself sit with it for a little while. Let your unconscious mind start working too, and notice what comes (now, or later). You see, you are pausing already, and it wasn't so hard, was it?

This little bit of introspection provides some framing. To build on those intuitions, I am going to give you three tools to help you to look more systematically at how you might start to build a practice of pause.

1. Design a calendar of pauses

The first is the calendar or diary. It is the tool we all use to organise our time. Whatever you call it, and whatever it might look like on the outside, every diary, whether paper or electronic, is the same in one important respect. It is laid out in some form of line which is chopped into clearly delineated chunks. A diary treats time as an objective, fixed, linear, one-dimensional commodity.

If you want to pause more then it is good to question this way of thinking. We have a lot of work to do here. It is a challenge to the tool-makers of the world — to give us more nuanced forms of diary that aren't so brutally linear. I encourage you to join in and mess around with your own calendar because it shapes how we conceive of time, and that is limiting. I am going to give you an example, as a start point, borrowed from Justin Wise (the Integral coach who gets his clients to go for walks).

Justin was inspired by musicians Amanda Palmer and Henry Rollins. When Palmer had a baby she couldn't play or tour; she felt like she was abandoning her career. So she borrowed an idea from Rollins. He alternates between what he calls 'inhale years' when he is absorbing new experiences and 'exhale years' when he is touring and working. Palmer used this idea to frame time with the baby as an 'inhale year'.

Justin took this language and decided to map it onto his calendar. He divided his time into 'inhale' and 'exhale'. 'Exhale time' is when he is teaching, writing or delivering work for clients. 'Inhale time' is when he is reading, studying, walking or spending time with people he just finds interesting. This adds another dimension to the regular calendar.

Justin combines 'inhale' and 'exhale' days in different ways to get the mix he wants over longer periods of weeks and months. He uses differently coloured Google calendars, where the colours represent how each kind of time feels to him. This allows him to see the kind of time he wants to have. He isn't always able to stick to it, and observes that 'exhale' time tends to invade 'inhale' time not the other way around. But even that still tells him something. It raises his awareness of what is happening and stops him from collapsing everything into an undifferentiated blur.

You could use these terms or, better still, invent your own. If you built your calendar in layers of time, what would the layers be? What different kinds of time would you identify? Instead of inhale or exhale you might have:

— *Tasks, learning, loves, distractions*

— *Mind, hand, body, heart*

— *Me, you, them, us*

— *Money, beauty, fun*

You could use colours or another visual device to represent each of these in your calendar. Pauses would appear not as gaps or holes, but as a switch from one kind of time to another. You would see if you have enough 'beauty' or 'fun' to balance out the 'money'. Or you might see it is time to do something with (or for) the 'hand'. Your calendar can become more than a list of obligations. With a bit of imagination, it can help you compose a life rather than organise your time, so that you spend it in a way that serves what you want, not what you are meant to want.

2. Personal pace layers

The second tool is also borrowed and adapted, but this time from the writer and environmentalist Stewart Brand. It is the idea of 'pace layers'. Brand originally came up with this while thinking about *How Buildings Learn* (he wrote a book of that title) and developed it further in *The Clock of the Long Now.*

The idea is that different domains or activities have different natural speeds — so while geology moves in millions of years, biology moves faster than that and culture is quicker again. Infrastructure takes decades, business and commerce have annual cycles, fashion is seasonal and tech start-ups are perhaps the fastest of all.

The organisation of this book into habits, design and culture is built on a similar observation — that our behaviour has layers, some of which move faster and change more frequently than others. What interests me here is using this schema to help you think about where you pause. Put simply, you can ask yourself what you could do to pause each day, week, month or year (or longer). Look at each layer and see where you can build in some pause.

As I have said, you can start to build a practice anywhere; however, it is more powerful if you are able to think about multiple layers and build a set of practices that weave together the different 'pace layers' of your life instead of just relying on one. Each layer will feed and reinforce the other. An annual pause might become part of your personal culture and give you the space to reflect on how to build new habits. Working in this layered way is a far more promising way to shape your life than the one-dimensional tussle over work-life balance.

So take some time (a minute, an hour, a day?) to think about each of these time-frames and where pause fits in. What do you do already that you could build on, or what might you begin? Don't be slavish about it and feel you have to cover all the bases, but do try to establish a practice of pause in at least a couple of different layers. If nothing else, it will get you thinking of time in a different, non-linear way.

3. The scanner

The third tool is a kind of scanner which builds on the idea of pace layers. It is a way to visualise how time *feels* to you, so that you can get a more detailed sense of where you might want to put some pause. It allows you to zoom in on any of the layers and get more texture.

You'll need a sheet of paper and a pen.

We'll use the binary notation of one and zero to represent two different kinds of experience.[4] The strong, sharp, straight 'I' will be used for busy, intense activity or time.

---

4 This notation is adapted from an idea developed by my friend Adam Morgan at eatbigfish, which he calls 'Pulsing'. He has generously let me use it here.

We will call that 'speed' for short. The round, empty 'O' will be used for calm, spacious experiences — we will call that 'space' for short. Pauses are in that category. So ones are speed, zeros are space.

Now take a period of time you want to think about: a day, week, month, season, year or lifetime. Don't agonise over which one — the exercise is quick and easy, and it helps to do this at more than one level of scale anyway. Just choose one to start with. Use as many ones and zeros as you like, don't rigidly allocate digits to each hour, or half hour. This isn't about the neatly delineated chunks of clock-time, it's about how it feels to you. So, you might put three zeros for a dreamy journey to work on a half-empty train to represent how that felt, even if it was only twenty minutes.

As an example, I am going to do my day yesterday. Without thinking too much, I go through the day and use ones and zeros to represent how yesterday *felt*.

Here is how my yesterday looks:

O I I I O I I I I I I I I I O I I I I I I I O O O O O O

The first zero is making coffee in the kitchen, in the early morning, while it was still dark. Then a burst of writing, a brief lull (for more coffee) before an intense series of business calls, bleeding one into another. Then, a short sit-down after lunch, more calls, straight into another period of writing and finally, glory be, an evening spent with friends in their newly built sauna, deep into the night.

As I look at it, what interests me is the shape and contrast (or lack of it). There is a fair balance of ones and zeros overall, but that long, barely interrupted stream of ones during the day didn't feel great. Maybe I could break that up more? Might that be a moment to introduce some kind of micro-pause?

I can't change the fact that I have to do the calls, but how about stepping outside for a moment between one call and another, just for a minute? If that helps I might establish a rule for myself that I can't start a new call until I have been outside. Even a momentary practice like that connects me to my body and the other intelligences it holds. Or I could do a moment of 'centring' — generating a quiet, inward stillness for a single minute, between calls. If I gave that a label — even if it's a cheesy one like 'Call Centre' — that could help me make it into a habit.

That long stream of zeros in the evening was great, and new. That's rare for me and the sauna was a wonderful way to recuperate after an intense day (I can still feel the effects now, the morning after). I can't do that every day but I can think about how to do it again, perhaps regularly. I might ask my friend Roland if we can establish a weekly pattern and make 'Sunday Saunas' a shared experience and part of the culture of our group of friends? [5]

Let's try a different level of scale — the year so far (it is September now). I am going to take a quick look back at my diary, to remind myself of what I was doing months ago, but only briefly — I am not trying to track things in detail.

Here is the year as I see it:

I I O I I O O O O I I I I O O O I I I I I I I I I I I

It started with an intense programme at Oxford, followed by a brief lull. Then concentrated work on the proposal for

---

5 I wrote this in early March and, in fact, this was precisely what happened. For the rest of the spring there were regular Sunday Saunas at Roland's house!

this book (the second burst of ones). Following that I had a couple of months of research, reading and interviewing people, which felt very expansive and open, hence all the zeros. Then back to Oxford, stepping into a colleague's shoes to take over the direction of a big programme, while trying to continue to work on the book. That was broken by a fabulous pause, sailing in the fjords in Norway. It was only a few days but had a huge effect, so I gave it three zeros. Since then, it has been a stream of ones writing this book, without interruption.

My eye goes to the long stream of ones that is the writing. Is that a good way to spend the summer? I wonder. Since it is hot I have always taken it for granted that things stop in summer, but this year it has been really productive for me. So next year I might plan a holiday in September and take on another writing project during July and August.

The particulars of my patterns aren't important — the idea is to illustrate how this exercise makes things visible and gets you thinking. Once you can see how your day (or month, or year, or life) looks you can decide where you want to focus your attention and how you might use pauses to change a pattern that isn't working. Note that there are no good or bad patterns, except as you define them for yourself. We are all different; you might thrive with a pattern that would frustrate me.

You could take yesterday, like I did, or last week, or last year, or next year, or your whole career or your future until retirement, or any other period you are interested in. You might do it retrospectively, to understand the past and make sense of it, or prospectively, to sketch out how you would like your coming day, week, month or year to feel.

Whatever the period, the exercise will suggest where you might want to build in some pause. The idea of practice is important here. As the word itself implies, this is about trying something out, not about getting it right first time. Look for start points, not answers: for 'a good thing to try' not 'the right thing to do'.

There is no way of getting it 'right' anyway, which means there is no way of getting it wrong either. So allow yourself to experiment. That will generate an experience of some kind or other. Notice what that experience is. If it was interesting, or useful, or valuable, or thought-provoking, or puzzling, or curious, or fun, or engaging in any way at all, do it some more. If not, try something else. To push hard, tense up or force things is counterproductive. That is the kind of attitude and energy that you are trying to get away from. If you have to push to make it happen, now may not be the time. Allow yourself the possibility of leaving it for later: to pause on the idea of pause.

However, while there is a lot of room for manoeuvre here, it is also important to accept that, at some level, conscious or unconscious, pause is a matter of choice. No one has a life so unrelenting that it is impossible to pause. If you think you are too busy, you are fooling yourself. This is not about how much time you have — as we have seen, a pause can be very short. Whatever your circumstances, there will be something you can do. You will have to work at it but if you really want to pause, you will find a way to do so. If you don't, you won't. It is totally up to you.

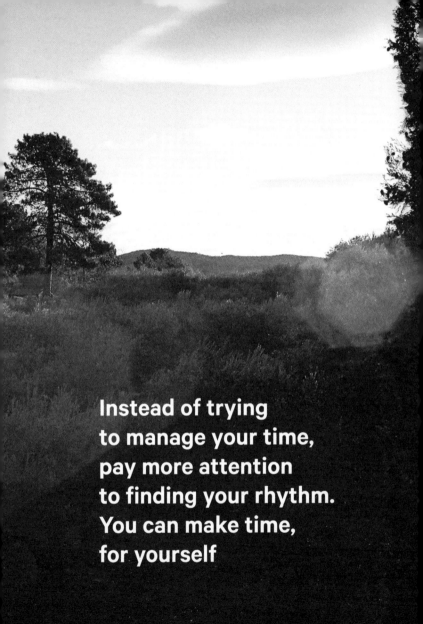

Instead of trying
to manage your time,
pay more attention
to finding your rhythm.
You can make time,
for yourself

7
Time to Pause

Exploring the idea of pause in depth has been fascinating. The chance to read, research, reflect and experiment with it has been both fruitful and fun. As a result, I am convinced that if you want to get more out of life, it is more useful to think about how and where you pause than to try and maintain a 'work-life' balance. Simple though that sounds, it has some far-reaching implications. It means changing our understanding of time and how we live in it. It invites us to think differently about how our minds work and encourages us to play around with how we shape and design our own experience. Which in turn means challenging some deeply held assumptions, including the idea that the more you do, the better it is.

To aspire to do as much as possible is an idea so widespread that it is taken for granted. This approach is logical enough and works well, up to a point. However, it has diminishing returns. The logic breaks down because trying to squeeze more and more in has negative consequences — most obviously stress and tension — that sooner or later outweigh the benefits, ultimately becoming self-defeating. More becomes less. If you are perpetually in a pinch, you are not your best self: you neither feel good, nor perform well.

'You run and you run to catch up with the sun but it's sinking, racing around to come up behind you again,' as Roger Waters put it.[6] The cycle can become vicious: it can lead to burnout.

Underlying this (flawed) strategy is a very powerful idea: namely that time is a scarce commodity, so you should use it efficiently. Benjamin Franklin did more than anyone else to popularise this notion, most famously in his dictum 'time is money', which is the ultimate expression of this point of view. That popularisation has been so successful that nowadays we rarely question it. It simply seems like the truth.

But it isn't. It would make sense if we were machines, but we're not. Our fulfilment does not derive from being as efficient as possible. Time, as we experience it, is not made up of regular, interchangeable units; we don't feel every minute, hour, day or year in the same way. Time is an aspect of our experience, not a commodity. When we are forced to stick to a regular metronomic beat, like a production line, life becomes dull and depressing. Such work is soul-destroying: it is much better done by robots (who, as far as we know, have no soul).

Good food, music, art, poetry, philosophy, science or sex are neither the result of, nor an expression of, efficiency. Beauty, joy, laughter, love, friendship and community owe nothing to it. Even an engineer seeking a solution to a mechanical problem expresses satisfaction in aesthetic terms when they land on an 'elegant' solution. Using efficiency as the measure of how we spend our time is misguided.

This is because we aren't linear. The human mind is vastly more complex than we can imagine, to a degree we

---

6 Pink Floyd: *Time*

are incapable of grasping. It has capacities that are contrasting, disconnected or even contradictory. We know this from art, science and philosophy, and from everyday introspection. The mind is not unitary or uniform: it is a many-splendoured, highly irregular thing.

This is reflected in the study of our psychology. Many different psychologists have proposed that within each of us there are separate minds, which perceive and understand the world in radically different ways. These different capacities of the mind are often strangers to each other. Freud gave us the hidden compartment of the unconscious. Daniel Kahneman has 'System 1' and 'System 2' for *Thinking, Fast and Slow* in his book of the same name. Carol Dweck, who invented the terms 'fixed mindset' and 'growth mindset', says everyone actually has both. Iain McGilchrist talks of *The Master and his Emissary*. Guy Claxton makes a distinction between the two in his book, *Hare Brain, Tortoise Mind*.

There are important differences between these theories — their authors aren't just using different words to say the same thing. Nonetheless, they all share the idea that there is more to mind than the conscious, rational thought that we normally refer to when we use the word. The implication is that, in effect, we have (at least) two different kinds of mind.

If so, then it is a shame and a waste to use only one of them. In a technologically driven world, fixated on efficiency, there is a risk that we do precisely that, and give undue importance to the most machine-like of our minds — the conscious, verbal thought we most identify with. The risk is greater because this dominant mode is 'vocal on its own behalf' and ignorant of the virtues of other kinds of mind. McGilchrist describes it as 'the Berlusconi of the brain' because 'it controls the media'. Convinced that the answers lie in more of its own kind of thinking, it pushes us to keep going, try harder and do more of the same kind of mental work. If you are a hammer the world looks like nails. If you are always in problem-solving mode, everything looks like a problem.

Which is where pause comes in. It is an antidote to the overwhelming and simplistic idea of nonstop activity. Pause acts as a switch to give you access to other aspects of your nature, to these 'other minds'. Just as yeast leavens bread, so pause lightens and enriches our experience. It allows us to think in other ways, using other qualities of mind: imagination, emotion, association, intuition, contemplation. It adds intensity of feeling, encourages us to perceive wholes as well as parts, gives emphasis to relationships not just objects and invites us to appreciate as well as analyse. Pause undoes the technology-driven flattening of time and gives it back some depth. It is re-creational. It gives you the chance to follow your mood, not the schedule. Pause is a portal through which you can access other layers of time that cannot be reduced, one to another. It can do this in a moment, or over a longer period.

For example, when you pause momentarily, you have the chance to check your knee-jerk reactions (to check in both senses: see what they are, and rein them in). You can notice your own internal state and interrupt the automatic, quick-fire responses that are normally in play (the fast thinking of Kahneman's 'System 1'). The bar across the door of the zendo, or the count to one before you enter a room, gives you the chance to access the more reflective mind (akin to Kahneman's 'System 2').

Johnnie Moore, founder of 'Unhurried Conversations', gave me a vivid example of this. Late one night, cycling

Pause undoes the technology-driven flattening of time and gives it back some depth

home, Johnnie rang his bell at someone who staggered into the street in front of him. The man, who was drunk, became angry too. He chased after Johnnie and confronted him at the next traffic lights. Johnnie paused for a moment and looked at the man. Somewhat to his own surprise, Johnnie found himself apologising instead of defending himself, or lashing out. Taken aback, the man then apologised as well and the scene ended up with them shaking hands, not fists. In retrospect Johnnie realised that he had inadvertently been practising for this. He had been working with some improv techniques designed to get beyond automatic responses. The pause had created enough of a gap for him to access that learning and get beyond his instantaneous reaction.

A longer pause provides a different kind of opportunity to engage a different kind of mind. It gives the intelligent unconscious — what Claxton calls the 'undermind' — a chance to have a crack at a problem, bringing a more associative, creative quality of thinking to bear. Two minds are better than one, especially when the two minds in question have such different ways of going about things. This is why 'consulting with your pillow' works. It is also why writers try *not* to stop at the end of a section of text, but to make a small start on the next one before they take a break. That way, this quieter mind is already working invisibly in the background on the next piece, in its own tangential, leisurely way. When you get back to your desk, it brings new insights that have bubbled up in the interim. It is this 'undermind' that impregnates the pause, leading to the more visible 'eureka' moments.

Since the 'undermind' doesn't 'own the media', its work is often invisible and other faculties take the credit, much in the same way that the contribution of quiet people in organisations is often ignored. This creative problem-solving capacity, and the pause it requires, is thus at risk to the 'efficiency' mindset, which sees anything resembling 'mind-wandering' as wasted time, rather than as a source of insight or new connection. Yet in any natural system there is always 'redundancy' or 'requisite variety' built in: stuff that isn't useful yet, but could be one day. My wife thinks our basement is full of junk: I see it as a source of material to solve problems that haven't occurred yet.

On a larger scale still, pauses also give you perspective and allow you to contemplate the kind of questions you can only approach obliquely. This is why the retreats I run are regenerative. People get a different sense of the issues they face, of what matters most to them or of who they really are. The switch away from everyday activity allows them to connect with the more contemplative side of their nature. The different rhythms allow them to perceive more subtle, diffuse and elusive stimuli, engage the imagination and weave more complex sets of connections. This quality of experience is simply not available in the midst of ceaseless activity. When Chris Riley spent the first day of a Reading Weekend 'watching his own anxiety', the frustration he felt was coming from the mind that was used to being busy. When he found himself solving problems he didn't know he had it was because a different mind was being given space, and came into play.

Thus pausing acts as a bridge from one mind, or one way of seeing and understanding the world, to another. It is not another task to squeeze on to your to-do list, but a switch that takes you from one mode to another. We are a composite of all these modes and a life well lived surely entails being able to experience each of them. Our lives may be a trance, 'a short pause between two great mysteries', as Carl Jung put it, but if so, then pausing can enable us to switch one trance for another and get a deeper sense of the endless variety that our lives can hold. Thus pause is not just a means to an end, but an end in itself. It is an opportunity to experience time, life and ourselves in a different way. There is more to life than getting things done.

In a practical sense pause is a simple idea with remarkable depth and variation. It gives you a single focus but a huge number of things to try, to suit your temperament or situation. It is easy to understand and remember. It can help you individually or collectively, at home or at work. Pause is neither a short-term hack to improve your productivity, nor a complicated step-by-step process that obliges you to redesign your whole life. It is a portal to a different understanding, appreciation and experience of time; one that is not linear. Time is no longer a line, chopped into thinner and thinner slices, but a series of layers, with depth and volume, that you can sink into or switch between, each with different qualities and properties.

This breaks open the hold that the efficiency mindset has on us. Instead of trying to cram more in, you focus on getting more out, by allowing yourself to pause and move between different qualities of experience. Stefan Klein calls this 'a new culture of time' and argues that 'by giving more life to our time, we give more time to our life'. Instead of trying to manage your time, you pay more attention to finding your rhythm. You can make time; for yourself.

Most people think of time as that which is marked by the clock. Time *is* 'clock-time' and we imagine it flowing, out there in the world, in a regular, uniform way: absolute and unstoppable. However, time isn't regular, or uniform, or objective, or 'out there' at all. Not according to Einstein, anyway.

Einstein fundamentally revised the way physicists think about time. He showed, mathematically, that time is relative. Asked to explain what this meant, he said: 'When you sit with a nice girl for two hours it seems like two minutes. When you sit on a hot oven for two minutes, it feels like two hours. That's relativity.'

His example was grounded in perception, but he was using that as a metaphor to describe the material reality of time. The variation isn't just perception — measure time closely enough and you discover it is for real. What Einstein's theories said, and subsequent observation has confirmed, is that time itself isn't constant, or objective, or universal, or absolute. Time is local. How it flows depends upon where you are in relation to other masses (particularly large ones, like the earth) and how fast you are going. There is less time downstairs than upstairs (seriously). There is no *one* single time. This does not mean there is *no* time: it means there are *lots* of times and none of them is the 'right' time. As physicist Carlo Rovelli puts it: 'The single quantity "time" melts into a spider-web of times.' Writer Jay Griffiths goes further: she asserts that 'the whole way time is described is ideological, if invisibly so' and observes that 'nature knows a million varieties of time'.

I find this liberating. It means that our perception is not so at odds with reality as we might imagine. It feels like an invitation (from the universe?) to shake off the straitjacket of clock-time and its mean-spirited partner, efficiency, and play around with time for ourselves, to make of it what we will. Pause is of that world, irregular and unruly, defying definition and beckoning each of us, in our own way, into a different relationship with time itself.

A pause allows
something to happen
which would otherwise
not occur, and you
never quite know
what that will be

Afterword

When you write a book about a subject like 'pause' you have both the opportunity and, I believe, the obligation to take up your own challenge and observe how you put into practice what you are writing about. During the process, I became sensitised to the phenomenon of pause and as a result found myself learning and benefitting on many levels. For me the project would have been worthwhile even if I had never finished the book.

There was a lengthy pause between the initial idea occurring, in February 2015, and it becoming a live project in January 2018. In that period it existed as what Steven Johnson would call a 'slow hunch', quietly gathering ideas and material around it. This allowed me to examine my thoughts from many angles and rehearse ideas with different people. I had time to see whether I felt it was really something worth doing. That long gestation period meant that once I started I was able to get going quickly.

The decision to start properly came in a pause, as decisions often do, namely a visit from Alex Carabi. The long walks we took powered long conversations, which were a break from my routine. It was on one of these walks that I gained the perspective necessary to see that the moment to start had come. I mean this quite literally: I was on a mountain top at the time.

Inspired by Alex's visit, I deliberately arranged a couple of other visits from friends who I knew would be good company, to fall during the writing period. I also scheduled a trip of my own — to Norway to go sailing. I wasn't sure how these would work, but they were 'forward anchors': time that was planned in advance when I would not be writing.

It turned out that these pauses worked in different ways: one I used to chew stuff over out loud, another to leave the book behind and let the 'undermind' do its thing. The trip to Norway was a classic example of how time opens up in a pause. It was only a few days but felt as deep and as wide as the ocean we were sailing on.

What I couldn't anticipate were the unplanned pauses that would occur along the way. Stepping in to cover for my Oxford colleague Tracey Camilleri when she was diagnosed with cancer took me away from the writing unexpectedly. That tested me and my thinking and yet allowed ideas to mature in a productive way. It also created a receptive space. It was while in Oxford that I came across Carlo Rovelli's book, *The Order of Time*, which turned out to be an important turning point. The shape of Chapter One also emerged during this period, while I was busy with other things — evidence that a change is indeed as good as a rest. If anything, rather than delay things, the time-out accelerated them and I didn't miss any deadlines.

The process of writing itself was also a playground for experiments with pause. I organised myself using what I dubbed the 'Darwin–Lubbock' method. This isn't a formula for settling the scores in a rain-interrupted game of cricket, it is a pattern of working in bursts, with pauses, based roughly on the way Charles Darwin used to work (his neighbour Sir John Lubbock, also a high achiever, apparently did something similar, hence the name). Darwin would spend an hour or two in focused concentration in his study, then go out for a walk, or potter about in his greenhouse.

I adapted this and created a practice of working in timed ninety-minute chunks, with breaks or other activity (often outdoors) in between. I aimed to do at least one and no more than three such sessions in any day. This helped me reconcile the demands of a long project with other commitments and domestic activity. It also stopped me from working too long and made up for the fact that I no longer have Cosmo, our dog, who used to take me out on walks when I got stuck.

It didn't always work. On one occasion it took a friend (in Utah) to point out that I needed to take my own medicine and take a couple of days off completely. Like anyone, I had all sorts of reasons why that wasn't possible, but I knew she was right and eventually took her advice to great benefit. Sometimes the pauses I had planned bumped up against pauses thrust upon me and the whole thing came close to stalling. Too much pause and nothing gets done.

In the act of writing itself, I also learned to rein myself in. I write on a computer and type quite fast, which has the risk that you head off in the wrong direction at speed. Just like being lost in a forest, retracing your steps is harder if you have been moving quickly. I learned to pause in the gap between words and phrases, my fingers hovering over the keyboard, advancing slowly, listening carefully to the space, trying to feel my way towards what wanted to be said.

To what extent I succeeded with any of this we will see, but I have no doubt that the book is better for having been an experience and experiment in pause as well as an exploration of it.

There is
more to life
than getting
things done

Resources

Many of the resources you need to pause come from within you, but external ones can help. Here are some of the books and talks that were useful to me in writing *Do Pause*. I hope you will find my own website and blog (*robertpoynton.com*) useful too.

Books

The Order of Time, Carlo Rovelli (Allen Lane, 2018)
   Poetic and thought-provoking — science writing at its best.

The Clock of the Long Now, Stewart Brand (Basic Books, 2000)
   The idea of pace layers is fascinating and powerful.

The Secret Pulse of Time, Stefan Klein (Lifelong Books, 2006)
   A more scientific look at time and timing.

Pip Pip, Jay Griffiths (Flamingo, 1999)
   A provocative and political take on time.

In Praise of Slow, Carl Honoré (HarperOne, 2004)
   A review of the Slow Movement.

The Empty Space, Peter Brook (Penguin, 1990)
   A director's take on how to avoid 'deathly theatre'.

A Philosophy of Walking, Frederic Gros (Verso, 2015)
   An exploration of the relationship between walking and thinking.

Videos, talks and websites

Unhurried Conversations: *unhurried.org*

Tom Chatfield — Ten commandments for critical thinking:
   search YouTube

Pico Iyer — The Art of Stillness: *search Ted.com*

Rotherhithe picture library: *sandsfilms.co.uk*

Olive-picking holidays: *bookculinaryvacations.com*
   (if enough of you get in touch with me, I promise I will organise a special *Do Olives* here in Arenas de San Pedro)

Long Now Foundation: *longnow.org*

About the Author

Robert Poynton divides his time between an off-grid, solar-powered house near Arenas de San Pedro in rural Spain and Oxford, where he is an Associate Fellow of Green Templeton College and the Saïd Business School.

In Spain, he hosts experiential events like Reading Retreats or the Creative Tapas Experience (a playful process of collaborative making) which act as pauses for thought. In a similar vein, in 2020 he co-founded Yellow, which is *all* pause — the events and retreats it hosts act as 'empty' spaces for reflection and learning.

His work at Oxford University is practical not academic: he uses the playful approach described in *Do Improvise*, his first Do Book, to help leaders navigate complex change. He has also worked with clients such as the BBC, Chanel, Merck, Unilever and Airbus.

He has spoken and led workshops at the DO Lectures, the Skoll World Forum, the d-school at Stanford University, Singularity University and Schumacher College.

His most recent book is *Do Conversation: There is no such thing as small talk* (2024).

He is married with three grown up sons. His wife runs an organic beef farm.

@robpoynton | *robertpoynton.com*

Thanks

First, enormous thanks to Miranda West, my editor, publisher and the founder of Do Books. None of the 'Do' titles would exist without Miranda, but in this case she has been even more important than usual. She championed the idea from the beginning and stuck with it over a number of years while my own enthusiasm waxed and waned. She was patient too, happy to pause on the project of a book about pause. I only hope that my efforts do justice to her faith in the project. To James Victore, for doing the cover. Again. I just hope what lurks behind it works as well as his wonderful image. For the images that act as pauses in the text, thanks to Jim Marsden, with whom I spent a lovely couple of days in Spain. David Hieatt can be a man of few words, but those he says, count. So, thanks to him for the subtitle. Once again, he has found a better way of describing what I am up to than I could myself.

Ella Saltmarshe, Gideon Todes and Nick Parker unwittingly kicked this project off. After an evening of improv exploring the theme of 'Pause', in the pub afterwards they each asked when the book was coming out. Thanks for that. It wouldn't have occurred to me otherwise.

I am very lucky to have an amazingly diverse number of people to learn about pause from, each with a different perspective, based in their own craft or discipline. At one point, when I was at a low ebb, I wondered if it was cheating to interview the people I knew, but then, in the course of one of the conversations, I realised I wasn't interviewing anybody at all — what I was doing was thinking together with them, and you do that best with people that you know, trust and love. So enormous thanks to all my wonderful thought partners: Adriana Sidicaro, Alex Carabi, Amanda Blake, Antony Quinn, Bruno Poynton, Chris Riley, Claire Genkai, Dan Klein, David Keating, Ed Espe Brown, Gary Hirsch, Helene Simonsen, Helga Schmid, Hilary Gallo, Iain McIntosh, Ioana Popescu, Johnnie Moore, Jon Stokes, Justin Wise, Kay Scorah, Les McKeown, Mark Barden, Neil Randhawa, Nick Parker, Phyllida Hancock, Thomas Sandberg, Tom Chatfield and Tom Hiscocks.

A special mention to Nick Parker, for being a constant companion throughout, providing a stream of thoughtful comments and advice on writing, much of it highly entertaining as well as useful. To Kay Scorah, who was the first person to draw my attention to how many different kinds of pause there are, and who has kept lobbing ideas my way. To Johnnie Moore, for always being available at the drop of a hat and for being so interested in the whole subject. To Alex Carabi for reigniting my interest when the project was languishing. Also a big thank you to confirmation bias, which, as Alex pointed out to me, works tirelessly for you when you are engaged on a project like this. I owe David Keating a startling number of the phrases in this book and it is all the better for them. Beyond that, I am also grateful for decades of conversation about how the ideas I am interested in intersect with his world, of which 'pause' is just the latest example.

Thanks to Jorge Alvarez for his companionship, humour and innumerable walks round the reservoir. To Adam Morgan for his permission and encouragement to use his own ideas. To Majken Askeland, Marius Filtvedt and 'New Excuse' for an unforgettable adventure in the fjords. To Tracey Camilleri, for her encouragement and for trusting me unquestioningly with the Oxford Strategic Leadership Programme. To Lynette Wood, for her enthusiasm towards the end of the process, when I could easily have wobbled. To my son Mateo for helping me think about how to make my ideas more visual.

For each book, I choose particular music to write to, so it becomes part of the process, almost part of the book. For this one it was Nils Frahm, who, unbeknown to him, has spent countless hours with me this year. I noted with interest that, much like Stefan Sagmeister, he took 2017 off as a way to prepare creatively for new work. He is, I think, a master of delay. As one of his fans said: 'I just spent six minutes listening to Nils Frahm, waiting for a chord progression ... but, boy, was it worth it.' So enormous thanks to him (and to my son Bruno who recommended him).

Writing gives you the excuse to read widely, which is a great joy. Of all that I read, three books stand out. Carlo Rovelli's *The Order of Time* is a gem that, fittingly, popped up at just the right moment. Stefan Klein's *The Secret Pulse of Time* showed me that my ideas weren't barking mad. Stewart Brand's *The Clock of the Long Now* — in particular the chapter on pace layers — is so deeply woven into my thinking that I barely notice, but I owe it and him a great debt.

To the people of Arenas de San Pedro, humble thanks for receiving us so generously nearly twenty years ago and for showing me how beautiful it can be to live at a different rhythm. And to the place itself, for the mountains, forests and streams which have become my home.

Finally, to the family. To my sons Bruno, Mateo and Pablo for being (surprisingly) interested in what I was up to and for putting up with endless hours of Nils Frahm. And finally, to my wonderful wife Beatriz, for the courage, patience and effort that has made the life we have together possible. Thanks also for letting me have the big table by the window as my own for such a long period. You can have it back now.

Index

Books in the series

Also available

Available in print, digital and audio formats from booksellers or via our website: **thedobook.co**. To hear about events and forthcoming titles, find us on social media **@dobookco**, or subscribe to our newsletter.